A Boy :
Digboi – A
Memoir

Crests, Troughs and Transitions

Debasish Ghosh

ISBN 979-8-88704-979-3

Contents

Opening Thoughts

When the idea of penning down my memories of a life, varied across many facets, first struck me, it was then little more than ticking off an item in a wish list. Gradually, this changed to be a more substantial effort, to a journal of life, a legacy of sorts to people who have made a difference to my life, for better or worse.

At the very outset, I must confess that the thoughts jotted down are, as they remain etched in my mind, 'to the best of my knowledge'. What does this phrase even mean? For thousands of years, we 'knew' that the sun goes around the earth. One fine day, a Polish scholar got the audacious idea of a heliocentric world, in which the earth revolves around the sun and not the other way around. Cometh other astronomers and mathematicians, and it was firmly established that it was the Sun, and not the Earth, that was at the centre of our system, the solar system.

In school, we were exposed to the 'phlogiston' theory. When magnesium was burnt, the weight of the residue was found to be more than the original weight of the magnesium itself. This was explained by magnesium having a component that had negative weight, phlogiston. Hence, on burning, this component was lost and the weight of the residue was more than the original weight of the magnesium. Negative weight? Are you serious? Yes, serious enough for it to be a perfectly plausible theory for hundreds of years. The list goes on and on.

Knowledge is transient and often, a function of time and space.

When we think of human interactions and relationships, covering bonds of love, friendship, hatred and indifference, we soon realize that they are far more complex than the simple and deterministic laws of physics and chemistry. What we 'know' can only be understood through a multi-dimensional function of time, persona and many other unknown factors. Over the last six decades, I have seen relationships change colour and shape, form and strength, not once but many times. Does that make us chameleons, in a sense? No, it is just that the human mind and heart resemble kaleidoscopes that keep generating different images, even if exactly the same stimulus is given, but at different points of time.

Finally, I offer my most sincere apologies to all whose feelings may get hurt by the contents of this collection of personal ramblings. I love each and every one of you very much, in different ways, or you would not have made your presence felt in my life, nor been made visible in these pages. It is just that some events have been less than savoury and a little hard to forget. Please forgive me if I have crossed any boundaries, especially in your mind.

Background

This journal covers a period of more than half a century; a period that has seen change on many different fronts. I strongly believe that without a reasonably good understanding of why, when and what events happened, our minds cannot do justice to the characters involved.

At the same time, let me emphasise that it is not my intention to be judgmental in any way; after all, who am I to pass judgment on characters and situations regarding which I have only an incomplete understanding, and recollection, in many cases?

1. Economic transition

Ever since I understood what money was, somehow it was always a five-letter word that seemed to be disrespectful, tainted and looked down upon by most around us. In the eternal duel between the daughters of Ma Durga, it was always a case of Ma Saraswati winning hands down over Ma Lakshmi, to the extent that prosperous business communities struggled, at least in our middle-class eyes, to command respect in social gatherings. Was this triggered by an in-built sense of inferiority that needed to be camouflaged, by emphasizing the virtues of education over the undisputed power of filthy lucre? I believe, that at least partly, this was true.

Not many of you will have heard the phrase 'he has a good job and earns a four-figure salary', a benchmark of affluence in those days, the sixties. Inflation notwithstanding, what this really allowed you was a lifestyle where everything was limited to the bare minimum. Daily travels were in impossibly crowded buses and trams, where little boys and girls had to cling on for dear life, many times a day. Sundays were looked forward to, only because that was the day when they could get a succulent piece or two of mutton. Clothes could be purchased but once a year, and that too in strictly pre-determined quantities.

If you got a visitor from foreign lands, kids would scramble to get cakes of soap, small pieces of chocolate, or a printed shirt bearing an overseas logo. Adults too, would look forward to souvenirs and trinkets, be it a ball-point pen made in the shape of the Eiffel Tower, or a key ring that had naughty images visible through an eyehole. Life was strictly bounded by rations and quotas, even in respect of dreams and expectations. People talk of the 'good old days' but I seriously wonder about how good those old days really were. Perhaps, I have become too materialistic; perhaps, time has widened my mental horizons and expectations.

2. Social Transition

Over the last few decades, societal structures have evolved immensely all over the world, with India being as good an example of change as any other part of the globe. Let me try and look back, based on my personal experience and from what I have understood, on how this has been reflected in our lives.

In the early fifties, my parents returned from their overseas stints in UK and Egypt driven by their passion for the newly independent country, the dream called India. The appeal of Gandhian values and Nehruvian visions of modernity, coupled with the rather unpleasant memories of having experienced life as second-class citizens in their own country under British rule, made this option look just right.

One fine day, my parents packed their bags and with a couple of toddlers in tow, returned to their homeland. What awaited them back here? After the initial euphoria, daily life quickly revealed its harsh side. Survival was all about how to do with as little as possible, and then to cut back even more. The only source of money was the humble income of an insurance agent (my grandfather) and the measly stipend-like salary that my father used to earn. Together, they had to support a family comprising my grandparents, my father and his four siblings, his wife and two infants. This grew to include my aunt and her children. Balancing finances until the end of the month was not just a feat, it was simply impossible. Life kept lurching along, from salary to loan repayment to fresh loans.

The glue that bound the family together was the insane amount of love and affection that every one of them had for each other. It was a tacit acceptance of the realisation that if they were to survive in this unforgiving world, they just had to be each other's source of strength. This was strength born, not out of muscles and bones, but from the heart. Every happy incident would be elevated to one of national importance; every crease on any forehead would rally the household around. You could say that they re-invented the spirit of 'All for one, and one for all'.

So it continued until 1960, when my mother got her first job as a resident doctor in Hindustan Copper Ltd, shortly after I was born. The only issue was that the posting was in a place called Ghatshila, about one hundred and fifty miles away. Remember, we are talking about the early sixties, when this was still considered to be quite a fair distance. Anyway, the monetary side being attractive, the family reconciled to our unit i.e. my parents, my brothers and little me, who was then just a few months old, moving out to this brave new world. My paternal grandparents, Dadu and Thamma, my Cairo'r Dadu (as we used to call my maternal grandfather, respecting an Egyptian connection that I never understood), uncles and aunts often took turns to come over and spend time with us. We were never deprived of either the loving affection of our grandparents or the support of our parents.

Life could not be better. Or could it? It surely could. Early in 1961, my father was transferred to Digboi by his company International Computers & Tabulators (ICT, later to become ICL, and then ICIM), where my mother was also offered a job as a Medical Officer at Assam Oil Company (AOC). For those who may not be aware, Digboi happened to have the world's second oldest oil producing well, second only to one in USA. It is widely known as the birthplace of the oil industry in India. Even in the pre-OPEC days, crude being located just beneath the surface meant that this company was flush with funds. Its cash flow problems were essentially one of how to limit its burgeoning coffers. This translated to largesse down its rank and file, in the form of generous salaries and allowances. As an AOC employee, my mother was in the right place, at the right time. Being an employee of a vendor to AOC, my father benefited too, but only to a limited extent.

Life for us changed out of sight, in a manner that nobody could have dreamt. We moved to a spacious bungalow, complete with servants at our disposal, a kitchen that ran a huge coal-fired boiler round the clock and a kitchen garden that was too big to be called that. I remember that my favourite childhood activity was playing in the kitchen garden, plucking fresh carrots and garden peas, washing them under the tap and munching on them. The fragrance and sweet taste of garden-fresh vegetables remain some of my most favourite childhood memories, even till this day. Fancy clothes, toys and chocolates arrived even before we could ask. Indeed, a far cry from our days of economic hardship in Calcutta.

One fall-out of this affluence, that often is an unpleasant accompaniment, was not allowed to come into our lives. I refer to the gradual estrangement between our core and extended family units. Continuing to be the responsible and dutiful members of the family, my parents considered it only natural that their financial well-being benefited not just us but them, as well. In fact, there rarely was a case of 'us' and ''them'; it was always 'us'. When my uncle needed a large sum of money to go to Switzerland to pursue his Hotel Management course, it was a given that he would approach his dear Boudi for the same. Whenever my grandfather needed funds for the house that he was building, my father was always the 'go to' person.

During our holidays, we would come to Calcutta in the veritable garb of Park Street's Santa Claus. There would be gifts galore for members of the house and lavish meals to celebrate every occasion. The entire household would look forward to our visits, and would carry us around in kid gloves, treating every wish of ours as a command. Boundless love coupled with generous hearts, backed by a total lack of monetary constraints; this was indeed pure bliss. Memories of financial hardships and deprivation were consigned to the dustbins of history.

Or so we thought. Unknown to us, underneath the glitter of a life beyond compare, lay festering the wounds of a marriage going desperately wrong; my parents' marriage. One February afternoon in 1969, it just exploded in our faces, catching us unawares. Before you could say 'Jack Robinson', we found ourselves, my father and his four sons, back in Calcutta, away from the centre of our universe, our mother.

The nightmare had begun. The only difference, between this and other nightmares we experienced, was that this did not get over in eight hours. It lasted for a little more than three years and took a lifetime to get over. The scars it left on us were so painful and real that even today, the effects are visible if one scratches below the surface of our smiles.

3. *Increased Mobility*

'Geography is history' is the line with which Motorola launched its Iridium services. Although it did not fare too well, the idea was representative of the times. Similar thoughts were also expressed by the noted futurologist and social scientist, Alvin Toffler in his classic, Future Shock and its sequel, The Third Wave. When I first came across these writings, I mistakenly thought that I understood what they meant. However, the deep significance of this transformational reality only began to sink in to my psyche, as I grew in years and was exposed to its various implications.

The economic and social transitions that I have tried to cover in the previous two sections of this journal had their genesis in the huge change that the entire world was witnessing, India being no exception.

Let us start with my grandparents. Thamma, my paternal grandmother, was the daughter of a well-to-do landlord. I have heard stories about their affluence, generosity and at times, ruthless behaviour towards their peasants, being answerable to none. I have also been told about my maternal grandparents who were rich enough to have ivory combs and bracelets as decoration pieces for the women of the house.

A common thread between both the households was that they had hired well-educated, but poor, boys from their neighbouring villages to come in, stay with them and impart at least a basic education to the young ladies of the house. If these teachers turned out to be good grooms for the girls, marriages were solemnized. I am not sure if this kind of informal adoption of bright young men into the households of affluent zamindars was common in those days, or not. Whatever be the social norms of the day, this meant that at least two ladies were transported, for life, from one economic and intellectual stratum to another. While the exposure to the three Rs of life did increase, this was also accompanied by considerable economic hardship for themselves and their fast-burgeoning families.

In time, this led to a deep-rooted bitterness towards life itself. Strangely, this resentment developed more in the husbands than amongst the wives, because they are genetically different. The wives had a remarkable ability to adapt to changing conditions that was way beyond the men folk, who held themselves responsible for the drastic climb down in their wives' lifestyle. I may be totally off the mark, but this is my personal hypothesis.

Added to this, were the horrors of a cataclysmic event called 'Partition'. Overnight, my Dadu had to pack his belongings and along with his wife, children, brothers and sisters, literally run for their lives all the way from Dhaka to Calcutta. In this strange new place, where he had nobody to call upon, he was forced to rebuild his life from scratch and support his large extended family. How he did it, how he survived, how he got everybody reasonably settled in life, I will never know.

During his twilight years, the cumulative effect of this unbearable stress took its toll on his mind, resulting in extreme stinginess, domestic violence with his wife and finally, mental ill health. Regrettable, but true. However, the almost inhuman strength shown by him, when many would have just crumbled, was remarkable. Staying together was the only way to survive, by allowing economies of scale to contribute to the home finances and spirit.

By the time the next generation came along, that is when my parents and uncles started to understand what life was all about, the perspective had changed. India was now an independent country fired by a dream of regaining its rightful place in the League of Nations (now the United Nations). I think that three factors combined to create this growing surge of restlessness amongst the youth of the early fifties.

One, having come to Calcutta, they were exposed to the lifestyles of the rich and the famous of this magnificent city; doctors, lawyers and engineers who seemed to live as if the world owed them a living.

Two, in the early days of Independence, travelling abroad, though time consuming, was ever present in their mental wish list, given the romance associated with long sea journeys, the charm of London (surely, it was the centre of the universe) and the timeless appeal of the Louvre just across the Channel.

Three, and this was probably the deciding factor, which convinced their parents to fork out the rather large amounts required. There was the widespread expectation that once a young man earned his degree, or even a vocational certificate, and rounded off his education 'across the seven seas', his future would be secured.

The youth of the fifties transitioned to the mid-level and senior-level executives of the seventies and eighties, who no longer considered the bounds of their hometown to be the Lakshman Rekha (the outer limit) of their dreams. If an opening came up in Bombay or Madras, Ghatshila or Digboi, it was just as viable an option as one in the central business districts of Calcutta (Esplanade and Dalhousie). Yes, this meant that there would be a few emotional farewells and promises to stay in touch, (some of which would be respected) but quality of life and financial well-being considerations easily conquered the pangs of the heart. As the larger cities became amenable to multi-cultural work forces, this phenomenon grew from strength to strength.

Fast forward to the nineties, when the mantra of LPG (Liberalisation, Privatisation and Globalisation) swept across the country, born out of a national economic crisis like no other. A growing foreign exchange crisis escalated to the point where, to pay for its oil bills, India had to pawn its family gold in February 1991. The entire country held its head down in shame, vowing that this situation shall never arise again. Just as Germany and Japan had done after the Second World War, the nation resolved to do whatever was necessary to be able to hold its head high at the earliest, to be able to take India back to its days of all-round glory, when Indian civilization was the cynosure of the world.

The brightest of Indian minds; engineers, doctors, IT specialists, financial analysts – they unleashed themselves on the rest of the world on a scale that was mind-boggling. Encouraged by foreign exchange rates that made remittances eye watering and enabled by a pro-active government that did all it could to ease the migration of labour, we suddenly had a situation where inward remittances grew out of sight. Foreign exchange reserves ceased to be a matter of national concern.

However, like in any seismic change, and surely this was no less than that, there was a price to be paid.

Overnight, the elderly folks in many families were deprived of their primary support systems – the emotional assurance and financial help provided by their middle-aged children and the adorable pitter-patter of the grandchildren they doted on. Most of those who chose to move away regularly sent their monthly support cheques, but this was more in the nature of alms, as a balm to their troubled conscience, whatever may have been the tone of increasingly infrequent conversations.

You only had to look at the elderly, behind their façade of smiling faces, to their soulful and pained eyes, to realize the angst of parents who have given up their lives and sacrificed their dreams to nurture their children, only for them to waltz away to the glamour of New York or the romance of Paris.

4. *Changing Values*

There is surely a lot to be said about the output of Bollywood, mostly uncomplimentary to say the least. Escapist fare delinked from reality; plots restricted to a handful of infinitely recycled themes etc. etc. Somewhere, in this miserable and mindless trash, we do find a few gems that stimulate our minds, strike a chord or two and make us ask uncomfortable questions. Baghban was one such movie.

While there could be debates about the treatment, the relevance of the subject itself is undeniable. The basic question asked by the film was this; our parents have given their all, all their todays and dreams for our tomorrows. When our tomorrows do arrive, when our parents' strength has ebbed and resources diminished, what right do we have to cast them away as flotsam, as deadwood, as rungs to be discarded once we have climbed the ladder of success?

I have seen this movie quite a few times. Every time, I have struggled to see it right to the end, only because it keeps asking me questions that I am not comfortable with, even today. I moved to Saudi Arabia in 2010, to fulfill my dreams in respect of my career, job satisfaction and the financial well-being of my wife and child. Of course, I did consult my mother before taking this huge step. However, I keep asking myself if this was a serious discussion or was it just information dressed up as a consultation? How would I have reacted if she had asked me not to move, as she was so dependent on Koli, Chiki and me for emotional support and succor?

Would I have engaged in an open-minded discussion on this topic, if I was not so sure that she would submerge her innermost desires for those dreams she knew that her son was daring to dream? Even after coming to Riyadh, did I do all that I could have, to stay as close to her as possible? The nagging voice just refuses to be silenced. I often take pride in trying to be as good a son, a husband and a father as I possibly can be. However, at the end of the day, we are mere mortals, and we do have feet of clay. We slip and fall, hopefully to get up on our feet again, most of the times.

Looking around me, I see people behaving in ways that appear strange, to say the least. Nowadays, graduates fresh out of college often get take-home pay packets that their parents could not even dream of, after decades of honest toil. Increased mobility of talent and wage arbitrage has also enabled many of them to spend time in the land of milk and honey or in the land of the rising sun, places that their parents could only imagine, having read of them in general knowledge books and travelogues. Based on this, these upstarts, these accidental beneficiaries of history, are elevated to a pedestal where their views on anything and everything, from geo-politics to social customs, from financial planning to health, overshadow those of others around. A family debate is often reduced to one where the 'yuppy' articulates his views and the rest find ways to concur with the same.

Where, I wonder, has the respect for grey hairs gone? Why is it that people, who have learnt and imbibed the fundamentals of science and technology, of human relationships, of tradition and culture, are politely forced to eat humble pie, bowing down to the power of the wallet? Is it not clear to even the mildly discerning eye that the road we are travelling can often be a slippery one-way ticket, if we keep ignoring and pushing aside the voices of reason, common sense and wisdom?

Agreed, that youth has the power of action, the dynamism of positive energy. It dares to question what has not been questioned, without carrying the baggage of imaginary limitations. It is capable of taking responsibilities much more than their previous generations did, sheltered as they were. However, there is much to be said for doses of moderation being injected into our lives. This will help us avoid treating life as if it is one extended bull run at the stock exchange, a run that has no end.

A Remarkable Ensemble

This is just a small selection of people whose imprints on my life have been indelible.

My Father, Prabir Kumar Ghosh (Baba)

My memories of my father are rather limited, but inspiring. For the first nine years of my life, he was the rather stern person, with ruggedly handsome looks, deeply resonating voice and for me, extremely protective. With my elder brothers, he did have a rather pronounced tendency to mete out corporal punishment, with my eldest brother being singled out the most; or so it appeared to me.

From what I have heard (mostly Mamoni), he was the very definition of a true blue incurable romantic. He declared his intention (or was it a decision?) to marry my mother when he was eleven and she was only five. Strong-willed and decisive, he had a lot going for him, to which you could add dollops of appeal stemming from his ability to play the pipes and being trained to join the Royal Air Force.

Academically too, he was very bright. In the prestigious Ballygunge Government High School, he was a class topper. Amongst his classmates and dear friends was my maternal uncle, Nantu mama, who had a rather distinguished career in Food & Agricultural Organisation, a wing of the United Nations. Unfortunately, financial constraints forced him to opt for a career over higher studies; in fact, more a job than a career, that was definitely not in keeping with his abilities. Such is life.

In terms of being the man of the house, he had few equals. He had a commanding presence that brooked no arguments. This was helped, by what Apu, a dear friend of mine, has aptly called a booming voice. When he spoke, others listened. When he made a decision, others followed. It was just as simple as that. A remarkable trait in him, to my mind, was the strong sense of responsibility and commitment to his principles. Two instances spring to mind, which demonstrate the nature of a man for whom walking the talk was the only way he knew.

In 1969, when his marriage was falling apart at the seams, Mamoni fell seriously ill. I still remember that day as if it was just yesterday. She had to be hospitalized immediately, for it was a life-threatening situation. Our house being close to the hospital (the same hospital where she worked), I kept looking in bewilderment as I saw Baba zip and zoom to and from the hospital, transporting Mamoni to the emergency ward, taking her essentials, change of clothes and what not. Only after all this was done, did he call us together to explain what had happened.

First things first, his dear Jharna had to be saved. How did it matter that she had already made it clear that they did not have a life together anymore? Love, this kind of pure and selfless love, is the stuff I read in novels nowadays or see in TV rom-coms. In real life? Not too often. Once she had progressed from the critical to the convalescence stage, she did not want to come back home as it was a strained environment. She decided to move in to the residence of the Chief Medical Officer, Dr. Edwards, for the rest of her recuperation period.

Although both of them realized, implicitly if not explicitly, that they had now come to the final parting of their ways, this did not change his behaviour towards her one bit. Every day, he would take us to Dr. Edwards' house where Mamoni would spend time with her children and discuss various issues with

Baba, I suppose relating to the near future, in the most civilized and normal (as normal as it could be) manner possible.

From Baba, I have learnt one thing. **You do not stop loving a person just because that person has stopped loving you.** Later on in life, I understood from Mamoni that **you do not stop loving a person even if for some reason, you cannot go on living with him**. These lessons are invaluable; it often takes more than a lifetime to imbibe these truths in your heart, in your soul.

Another incident that I recall, though nowhere as dramatic, occurred towards the middle of 1970. Pipi's (Baba's youngest sister) marriage had been fixed for 30th May. As the primary earning member of the extended family at New Alipur, and being the eldest brother of the bride, he was carrying the financial and other responsibilities of the event single-handedly on his shoulders, broad and strong as they were.

Those days, I used to wait for Baba to come home from work. Only then, would I have dinner, regardless of the time. One day, a couple of weeks before Pipi's wedding, the night kept on getting late but there was no sign of Baba. We are talking of 1970, when leave alone mobile phones, we did not even have a landline. As the clock kept ticking away the minutes, we started getting nervous and jittery, wondering what had happened. Fearing the worst, all kinds of unspeakable thoughts started to cloud our minds.

Close to midnight, we heard the sound of our car and we heaved a collective sigh of relief. After a while, we saw Baba climb up the stairs to the first floor, in extreme pain. The index finger on his right hand, his driving hand, was in a hard plaster.

What had happened? Earlier, as he was preparing to wind up for the day, pre-occupied with the million things that needed to be done for Pipi's wedding, carelessness and exhaustion got the better of him. His finger got stuck in the jaws of a rolling machine. In no time, his index finger was reduced to splinters, if not pulp, in a few places. Fortunately, people around him could stop the machine and extract his finger before taking him to the hospital. Obviously, the finger was still painful, and strong painkillers and sleeping pills should have been administered, to ensure that he got rest and a good night's sleep.

He refused to take any of the stronger medication that would make him dizzy, as that would mean him not driving back home and possibly staying for a couple of days in a nursing home. How could he do that, when so much still remained to be done for the biggest social event in our family for well over a decade? How could he not come home, knowing that his aged mother and 10-year-old boy would stay up the whole night, if required, waiting for him to return? No, he had to drive with that smashed finger in a cast, regardless of how painful it was. This was the man Baba was, a real man in every sense of the word.

On the other side, he had a persistent streak of insecurity regarding his wife which he sought to cover up with his violent behavior, something that was totally unacceptable, regardless of the provocation. Ultimately, he paid the highest price for this fatal flaw in his character, an Othello-esque anger that at times, found expression through his muscles.

Here, I must mention something that was special about him. Never, not once, during the last three years of his life that he spent without his beloved wife, did he have anything negative to say about her, at least in our presence. He understood the meaning of, and practiced, compartmentalization when all around him did not even have the foggiest idea of what it was all about. These people did not know that it was almost criminal to poison the impressionable minds of young children against their creator, their life giver, their mother. For all his faults, **he was a true man who could never belittle the mother to her children**, regardless of whatever differences he may have had with his wife. Baba, for this alone, you will always remain an idol of mine.

At the early age of forty-seven, when most people are getting primed for the best years of their lives, he left this world, heartbroken and insecure of how things would shape up for his children. He need not have worried too much on this account. In his wife, in the mother of his four boys, there was this super strong survivor, this lady we had the privilege of calling our mother, who would make sure that we could reach for the stars.

My Mother, Jharna Maitra (Mamoni)

I am tempted to start this introduction of Mamoni on the lines of the opening words in Love Story. 'What do you say about a woman who died? That she loved Beethoven. And Bach. And me.'

She was born to take care of people around her, in as many ways as possible. As her father was always bit by the bug of wanderlust, she would be the one to ensure that her father's life stayed on the rails even when they moved out of Calcutta to various places including the hills of Kasauli. Her father's irresistible need to stay on the move was probably, an escape mechanism, from the burdens of parenting seven children and a daughter-in-law, as well.

(An interesting side note: It was in Kasauli that my grandmother developed a rather close friendship with a lady, whose husband was the Chief Engineer of Kasauli Power Company, through their common interest in poetry. This lady's

grand-daughter incidentally is Aditi, my partner in life. Funny, how life takes you around tight circles!)

When she was just a little girl of nine, she lost her mother. As she blossomed from childhood to youth, and in spite of not having her mother to shepherd her through the formative years, her persona took on a wide range of hues. Apart from being one of the most charming persons to be with, she was a striking beauty with a top-class brain. If that was not enough, she was also a diligent and serious student. During her studies in England, one of her professors would comment on her atrocious and illegible handwriting (note, no almost, her handwriting was truly indecipherable!) that the reason for her less than perfect calligraphic skills was that her fingers could not keep pace with her mind. He advised her to write in as big and bold letters as she could and not worry about environmental damage caused by deforestation.

To remember Mamoni, and not discuss her resilience, would be a travesty of sorts. Let me recount just a couple of incidents to give readers a flavour.

I go back to early 1954, when she was living in comfort, in Alexandria. Baba was not in town at this point of time. A spacious bungalow, a retinue of domestic help, and fresh orange & carrot juices to keep the skin glowing; this was just a sampling of life those days. Although there were simmering differences between General Nasser and General Naghib, it was widely expected that things would blow over soon. Suddenly, General Naghib was arrested and General Nasser took over complete power. Mamoni was given exactly three hours to pack two bags as all British subjects needed to be evacuated before the Egyptian army came and ransacked the city of Alexandria. She was picked up in a small trawler before being transferred to a large ship, which was, in fact, a whaler.

As the ship steamed out of Alexandria port, she watched in horror as her beloved home went up in flames.

The next morning, the evacuated passengers were served coffee and biscuits on the upper deck. Down below, a massive whale was being cut open with an electric saw. Mamoni was absolutely fascinated by this sight. Gone was the terror of being evacuated with a couple of hours' notice and two bags, gone was the horror of seeing her home torched. Being the young wide-eyed girl that she was, just twenty-three years of age, the only thing that she could see was this gigantic mammal, being cut across longitudinally, its innards bursting open like orange pods on either side as the massive saw made its way across. All else was forgotten, was history.

For the next episode, we will need to move forward to 1968, shortly after she had met Kaku as Baba's boss, nothing else. It was probably this incident that sparked the relationship between the two, but that is only my fertile mind's conjecturing.

Digboi was surrounded by large tracts of open forests, in which herds of elephants, leopards, snakes and other wild creatures were commonplace. At the same time, it was rich in bamboo, fruits and vegetables. Many of the local villagers earned their livelihood by foraging and from time to time, they came into contact with the wild residents of the forest. On the day we are talking about, a young woman was gored by a tusker, right across the stomach. Fortunately, there were others in the vicinity who made enough of a racket to drive the elephant away, but what could be done about this woman who lay on the jungle floor, whimpering in pain, with her entrails strewn all over? Somehow, they managed to bring the woman, with her intestines hanging out, to the hospital where Mamoni was the only doctor on duty at that time. Kaku, for some reason, was also there, which turned out to be providential.

The first thing that needed to be done, if the lady had to have even a chance in a million to survive, was to get the intestines back in her abdominal cavity. Having no other choice, Mamoni requested Kaku to help her in this. Dazed as he was, I suppose that his manly ego did not allow him to turn down this request by the beautiful lady doctor in front of him. Rolling up his sleeves, he got to work. He started picking up the intestines from the floor, washing them in an antiseptic solution and passing them on to Mamoni who carefully stuffed them where they belonged. Not that there was any realistic chance of the woman surviving this procedure, but they still had to give it their best shot. Miracle of miracles, the woman did survive.

And I think, a romance was born.

I could go on and on, eulogizing her endlessly, but let me stop here. It is not that she did not have her flaws; she was human too. With all around pampering her no end, she did have more than a streak of vanity and loved to be surrounded by those who would make her feel even better. She did not suffer fools easily, especially in her professional front. In the operation theatre, she was not averse to delivering a sharp kick to members of the operating team if they committed a blunder. She also had more than her fair share of admirers, and this did become a major bone of contention with my father.

With her children, she was, frankly speaking, little less than a living god. Borda and Mejda would crawl all over her whenever they could, saying that don't you know that baby crabs crawl all over their mother, you are our mother crab.

When Mejda was struggling with Chemistry in high school for a year or so, she sat down with him and explained the basics and fundamentals so well that he topped the class in the final exams, to the total surprise of all.

Due to an unfortunate three-month long rail strike in 1974, I returned to Hyderabad after my annual vacation in Calcutta, totally unprepared for the Class Ten Board exams. So far behind the class was I that my teachers advised me to consider dropping a year to avoid getting disgraceful numbers. How did Mamoni react? She was not capable of teaching me as the subjects included History, Geography and Maths, not exactly her forte. Regardless, she took it upon herself to help me make up for lost time by sitting with me virtually round the clock for the two months that were left, encouraging me, cajoling me and challenging me to push the boundaries. What was the result? I came out close to the top of the class; my teachers and fellow students were left picking up their chin from the floor.

Simply said, there was nothing that she would not do, could not do, for her children.

Before signing off on this all too brief a pen sketch of this amazing lady, I would also like to mention a not too well-known side of Mamoni, the poet. It started with her dabbling in simplistic topics expressed in basic structures, which she would share mostly amongst her friends in literary circles. Gradually, encouraged by the feedback and valuable suggestions obtained, her poetic output, in English and Bengali, was enhanced in both content and structure. She had a number of diaries filled with spontaneously written poems, the subjects ranging from a love poem to Kaku to her frustration about systemic and societal constraints. My understanding of poetry, and that too Bengali poetry, is rather limited; else, I could have expanded on this with greater clarity than I have been able to.

My second father, B C Maitra (Kaku)

Not too many people are blessed with three parents; we brothers definitely were. It took us time, some a little longer than others, to realize this undeniable fact. To simplify the narrative, let me start at the beginning.

Earlier, I have tried to outline the gradual collapse of my parents' marriage, with things having deteriorated to the point where it was a question of when, rather than if. At this point of time, came Kaku into our lives. Obviously, the chemistry between my mother and him sizzled, for otherwise they would never have been able to, or wished to, embark on a journey together that lasted no less than thirty-seven long years, till death did them part. For thirty-three years of this remarkable partnership, there were four other players in the field, the four children.

Two of us, Baby and I, were for all practical purposes, their children while our two elder siblings – Igloo (Borda) and Bigloo (Mejda), shared a more adult relationship with them. This was partly due to the difference in our ages but mostly a reflection of the much stronger bonding and responsibility that they felt towards us as compared to our elder brothers, who were well into their teens and had far more independent minds. It was also due to a greater sense of being let down they had, that made it difficult for Borda and Mejda to rebuild bridges with Mamoni and Kaku. I must confess that I too struggled, for a long time, to accept him in my father's place, but more of that later.

What he did to restore sanity initially, and then stability and security in our lives, give us a strong identity and much more, is the stuff modern day fairy tales are made up of. While I have tried to recount certain episodes of mind-blowing demonstration of love, responsibility and affection, the sum was much greater than the parts.

How do you put in words the thoughts of a child, reduced to being a penniless orphan being transformed overnight into a proud student of one of the most elite schools in the country, rubbing shoulders with the sons of the city's glitterati, cognoscenti and industrial barons? Of children who did not know where their next meal would come from, being transported to a world where they had to choose between fragrant biryanis and delicious kababs for dinner?

This was not because they were awash with money, but because they realized how deprived we had been of the simple needs of life – mental, emotional, financial and social. Both of them were determined to erase the scars of the 1969 to 1972 period, applying as much salve as they could.

All said and done, Mamoni was our mother, who had always loved us beyond compare. What about Kaku? He was just a young man, hopelessly in love with his glamorous, uber-qualified wife with whom he was just about starting to build a life together. It would have been easy for him to distance Mamoni from us, or at least try to (not sure if she would have acquiesced) to have her all to himself. In fact, it was probably in the innermost recesses of his mind to start a family 'of his own' with Mamoni.

This is where his greatness lay, and I do not use this word lightly, and his nobility came to the fore. He never saw us as anybody other than a family 'of his own'. Every joy of ours was an occasion for him to celebrate; every hurdle faced was one to be overcome together. There are a few issues on which I differed with him, but they fade into complete insignificance when I look at the big picture.

Without him in our lives, we would have been debris drifting aimlessly in some fetid, putrid brackish water pond in a state of total disrepute and namelessness.

My Eldest Brother, Partha Ghosh (Borda)

Borda, my dear eldest brother. The brother with whom I have spent the least amount of time, and this I consider to be my big loss. In Indian society, the eldest brother is normally the Gabriel Oak (*Apologies: Far from the Madding Crowd, Thomas Hardy*) of the family, the stoic who takes on the bullets that life can shoot, who shelters his younger siblings from all the rain, thunder and lightning that there is around. I have seen the unbelievably strong bonding he has with Mejda (more of that later), giving me a flavour of what I have probably missed out on.

Born in London, he was a star, a lady-killer right from the cradle. Mamoni's friends would come to visit her and be captivated by the impossibly good-looking baby. Effortlessly, he would win them over with his irresistible charm even then. Did the ladies who crossed his path later on in life, from teenagers to dowagers alike, ever have a realistic chance of not going weak in the knees? I seriously doubt that.

At the age of two, he came to Calcutta and immediately asked that an igloo be built, to help him cope with the heat and humidity of the tropical city as opposed to the temperate climate of London. All around him found this to be so endearing that they promptly created a nickname for him, Igloo, and in the process, started a naming system for the rest of us; Bigloo, Chotloo and Babyloo. Funny, how some things just get going out of a chance remark from the mouth of a babe.

As he blossomed, so did the prank quotient within him, ably assisted and fueled by his lieutenant, my Mejda. Being separated by only eighteen months in age, these two were inseparable, like the pods in a pea, in spite of being different in all possible ways. If Borda was the leader, Mejda was the follower. If Borda was the brawn, Mejda was the brain behind most of the escapades. Where Borda would be at the front end of operations, Mejda would be looking after the logistics from the bunker, so as to speak. If things went wrong, most tragically for Borda, he would normally be the fall guy while Mejda, more often than not, would be the one slinking out through the rear gate of troubled spots.

Overall, the two of them formed quite a formidable pair, especially in the fields and homes of Digboi. I will try and bring to life some of their memorable adventures, but I doubt that words will be able to capture the sheer audacity of what they did, which others could only marvel at (if you were in their age group) or tear their hair out (if you were unfortunate enough to be at the receiving end of their pranks).

Borda faced the brunt of Baba's anger, corporal punishment and all, far more frequently than any of us. When we look back on the frequency and severity of the punishments meted out to him, we wonder if there was any underlying cause. Being a father myself, I cannot imagine raising my hand in anger on my daughter; how could he be so violent with his son, and that too his first-born, his primogeniture? Beyond my limited powers of comprehension, I must confess.

Moving forward, when my parents decided to call time on their marriage, Borda was hit the hardest amongst us for more than one reason. First, being the eldest, in his teens and on the verge of adulthood, he understood the issues involved and the viewpoints of his parents, especially Mamoni whom he loved more than life itself, more than anybody else did. Just a few days back, I was having a chat with Boudi who mentioned that even today, after all these intervening decades, Borda still has quite a few unresolved issues and feels the pain.

Secondly, he had to stay an extra year in Digboi, all by himself, while the rest of us moved to Calcutta as he was in his final year at school, preparing for his Higher Secondary exams. As an aside, let me mention that he did rather well in his Board exams, getting a 'Letter' (more than 80%) in Maths, no less, and securing a First Division overall. Given the turmoil that his impressionable mind was going through, this spoke volumes; not only for the steel in him, but also the discipline instilled over the years. Borda, I may never have articulated this before, but I take my hats off to you. One factor that played out in his favour, during these excruciatingly difficult times, was the love and affection he got from our next-door neighbor in Digboi, the Raha family.

After his Board exams, Borda joined us in Calcutta. The absence of Mamoni and the constant sniggering around us, friends and relatives (with the sole exception of Baba) alike bad mouthing our dear mother without even pausing for breath, was too much for him. This was the same person, who until recently could never put a foot wrong; such are the idiosyncrasies and vicissitudes of human nature! Eventually, all this pressure and negativity took its toll. A person who could glide effortlessly through the Board exams in the midst of his parents splitting up, failed to get through even the preliminary stages of his Bachelor of Commerce degree in a rather non-descript college, City College. This was a place where students struggled to spell the word 'academics' but excelled in the lifestyles and love lives of movie stars and local politicians. Smoking cigarettes, drinking liquor, experimenting with weed and hash were the status symbols of this breed; a one-way ticket to nowhere was got and the downhill journey was ready to be embarked upon.

31

As awful as it may sound, if Baba had not passed away as suddenly and quickly as he did, I shudder to imagine what would have happened to us. Not for nothing is it said that if the Sun is the centre of the solar system, the mother is the centre of a functioning home. How dysfunctional it can be in her absence; we have understood only too well. It is something that we would not wish even on our worst enemy, and that is no exaggeration.

After Baba left us for a much better world, in March 1972, Borda and Mejda continued to stay in Calcutta in our 'ancestral home', on the strength of the financial support provided by Mamoni. Another aside on our 'ancestral home'; we believed that it was so, till we were brusquely informed by our loved ones, that *we had no rightful claim to it*, regardless of the fact that it was built primarily on the contributions sent by my parents from Digboi.

After drifting rather aimlessly in this way for a year and a half, Borda decided that it was finally time to rejoin the mainstream of life, to join the rest of the family in Hyderabad. Mejda had already come over after his Senior Cambridge exams.

A brief idyllic period followed. Borda and Mejda were totally bowled over by the love and affection showered on them by Mamoni and Kaku. They also saw for themselves how well their younger brothers had integrated into a new life with refreshed and revitalized identities. Borda gained admission into the prestigious Nizam College while Mejda joined Science College.

Life seemed to be getting back on the rails.

However, deep within, there was still a residual resentment in Borda's mind about Kaku taking Baba's place, and this was only to be expected. Speaking from my own experience, I know that it took the better part of three to four years before I could even accept the two of them sharing the same bedroom. There, I have said it!

Come August 1974, and Mamoni's brother's family, who were based out of Rome, came to visit us for a couple of weeks. My maternal uncle, Nantu mama, was then working with FAO. The glamour quotient of their family was higher than any other we knew. Nantu mama was an absolute dasher, good looking, dressed to kill, bow tie and all. His wife, Ruth Aunty, was always elegantly turned out, coiffure, chiffon and pearls to boot. Loya, their eldest daughter, who was just a few months younger than Borda, had the killer looks of an Italian diva. They had two sons, Alok and Amit, who were in the same age group as Borda and Mejda.

Between the five of them and their associated glamour, they convinced Borda that he was only frittering away his talents in the backwaters of Hyderabad, as glitzy Europe was just waiting to transport him to worlds unknown. Being born in London, both my elder brothers had the advantage of being able to choose their passports; Borda opted for the red one of United Kingdom. Within three months of their arrival in Hyderabad, Nantu mama's family managed to separate our dear Borda from us. Mamoni was not one to get upset for a long time easily, but I do not think that she forgave Nantu mama for creating this chasm in our family, ever.

Reaching London, life was hardly what he had expected. Trials and tribulations awaited him at every turn, in so many shades, that I have requested Borda to jot down his colourful experiences and escapades, his trials and tribulations, in a diary for all to savour. Just to give a sneak preview, it includes being let down by close relatives, bar brawls, getting beaten up to an inch of his life by skinheads, feeding meat to lions to earn a living, restoring castles, cooking food and serving it to his guests for months on end; the list goes on and incredibly on.

However, the point to note is that in spite of all the challenges faced by him in UK, he refused to accept failure and neither was he willing to come back home defeated. For eight long years, he did his utmost to create his own success story before coming to Calcutta to visit us in early 1982, firmly established on his own feet, by sheer grit and determination.

A never say die attitude, that has always been your hallmark, dear Borda.

My second brother, Shankar Ghosh (Mejda)

From the day he was born in chilly, blizzard-hit London in November 1954, life was a struggle for Mejda. Born with six fingers on each of his hands, he needed to undergo cosmetic surgery within days. This was a courageous decision taken by Mamoni to avoid him being labeled as some kind of freak throughout his life. Just a harbinger of things to come.

Being Borda's partner-in-crime during their teenage years in Digboi, he received his fair share of physical punishment from Baba, though to be perfectly honest, Borda did get a little more than his. He was finicky about food; after dinner, underneath his plate often lay a ring of mashed vegetables, fish or chicken if it was not tender enough for his palette. He would be reprimanded for this behaviour, but it did not seem to leave any lasting impression, for every meal was a repeat of the one before.

After the days in Digboi came to an abrupt end, he had to take on far greater responsibilities, especially during the year when Borda was still in Digboi for his Board exams. Not only did he have to be the big support for Baba during his days of total solitude and quiet despair, he also had to take care of various household functions such as drawing money from the bank, paying utility bills and other stuff that I was not aware of. What I knew only too well was that he would accompany me to school and back, that involved four trips a day on overcrowded buses and suburban trains. He would also find ways & means to keep me reasonably chirpy and focused on academics rather than all the messy affairs of difficult circumstances.

Due to financial stringency, Baba would give him exactly Re 1.00 every day to cover the bus fares for the two of us (Re 0.15 New Alipur to Esplanade, Re 0.10 from Esplanade to Moulali and the reverse for the return journey); nothing more. Imagine the climb down from the lifestyle we were used to, for nine years, in Digboi.

In our school, there was a small shop set up in a garage where this vendor would sell delicious potato rolls and other tasty goodies, which we would yearn to eat, but could not. Across the school, there was a small shop that sold the most divinely scrumptious hing kachori for Re 0.10 a piece that we could only salivate on as we passed it on the way to the bus stop. Mejda guided me into the art of sneaking WT (without ticket) rides on bus journeys, and the money thus saved would finance our occasional potato rolls and hing kachoris. There would be days when I would be disheartened by the unfairness of life, and there would he be, literally and figuratively, picking me up, lifting my spirits, assuring me that tomorrow is another day; that life can and definitely would, only get better.

While being this source of constant encouragement for me, he was fighting his own internal demons. In Class Nine, he failed to clear his final exams. As you can imagine, there are few events as destructive of your ego and self-esteem as having to bring home a report card that spelt out in bold red letters "Failed. Not promoted." This was the day that he came closest to disintegrating, to just giving up on life.

Even in this totally shattered and demoralized frame of mind, he had the sense of responsibility of taking me to the local railway station and putting me on the train that would bring me home without the need to change buses. Then, he took a suburban train to a few stations away, got down, and sat there, looking vacantly out to space. I am not sure what transpired there, but after a couple of hours, he regained his composure. He took the return train and came back home, ready to face the insults and mockery **but determined to never run away from the challenges of life ever again**. In this context, if I remember correctly, it was Baba who understood and fully empathised with what he was going through and to the extent he could, made things as easy as possible.

This amazing grit, determination and resilience would come to epitomize what he is, and always will be. Just to give a few examples, he refused the soft option of taking a British passport to be able to honour his personal commitment to the cryogenics and space research dream of resurgent India. He stubbornly stuck to his entrepreneurial dream even when the senior-most and technical lead member went back on his word to break away from Asiatic Oxygen to lead their start-up, Shell-N-Tube.

Along with his brother of another mother (that is the only way that I can describe you, dear Munjal bhai) they continuously ploughed back the earnings of their love child, Shell-N-Tube, into the firm rather than fatten their personal coffers.

I cannot sign off on Mejda without mentioning his two passions, wild life and photography. If an occasion did present itself for the two to be combined, you had the very prescription of '32 all out' on his face. It all started with a hand me down Praktika camera he got from Borda in 1982; and then, there was no looking back. From stunning landscapes to positive-energy filled portraits of rural women and glam-sham friends, from majestic elephants to raging waterfalls, every subject of his photographs seemed to be looking directly at the lens, full of expression and character. As time passed, so did the technological range of his photographic equipment, leading to his photographs moving from the excellent to the classic.

Amongst his prize pictures, I would like to make a special mention of a few wildlife moments captured in time – the black leopard sighting in Kabini reserve forest, the terrifying sight of an elephant in *mast* (heat) bearing down upon him, and the fierce growl of the leopard baring its fangs in full glory. If he had not been such an impassioned cryogenics engineer, the world of photography would have been considerably enriched by his contributions. He is indeed a role model for a first-generation entrepreneur, technical visionary and ultimately, a person who most of us can use as a textbook, a reference point for determination, for never taking the easy way.

In my school days, I read a line in Reader's Digest 'A brook gets crooked by taking the path of least resistance. So do men.' – Lord Tennyson.

Mejda, you are anything but a brook. You do not have a single crooked bone in you.

You make me proud to be called your brother.

My youngest brother, Prasenjit Maitra (Baby)

Baby, we remember you.

Born in the lap of luxury, you came in to our lives, straight from Woodlands Nursing Home to the regal lifestyle of the oil township of Digboi. Silver spoons and chocolates surrounded you every which way.

All too soon, that paradise went for a toss. Being too young to be separated from your mother, you moved for a while to Mumbai and even had Rajesh Khanna attending your birthday party. Not too bad for a starry-eyed six-year-old. This too, did not last. Back to the harsh impossible environment of Calcutta, you faced discrimination that we normally associate only in movies, horror movies.

Fortunately, this phase was short-lived. You and I moved on, to what I firmly believe, was the most wonderful phase of our lives. A stable and loving family, with joy and laughter restored, great friends; they all combined to make it the most wonderful environment possible to grow up in. Paradise lost, paradise regained – in short.

Six years later, we moved back to a city called Calcutta. Why, I will never understand. You faced challenges, more than the rest of us put together. Life, in general, and formal academics in particular, treated you badly. You also developed grand mal, the seizure accompanying form of epilepsy, that marked you out to be different, and in a not nice manner, from others around you. To make things worse, it also adversely affected your formal studies.

Then came JCMC, Jodhpur Circle Medical Centre. It was the culmination of Mamoni's long-term dream to have a place of her own; a nursing home where she could be free to pursue her vision of medical care, her way of providing life support to the poor and needy, subsidized by earnings from the well-heeled members of society. It gave a new meaning to your life, encouraging you to blossom in a manner that frankly, many of us did not think possible.

But you did, and how! You grew to be the most trusted and reliable deputy to Mamoni's dream, working hours that were long and intense, with not a single murmur. You also found the love of your life in the apartment overlooking JCMC and with more than a fair share of drama, brought Shampi into our lives. The sister we had always craved for, but never had.

Fate refused to keep smiling on you for too long and showed her capricious face once again. Just as suddenly as Shampi walked into our lives, she walked out. And I suspect, along with herself, she took away your dreams. Wistfully, you would look to the skies, to the same Garden Apartments where your dear wife had returned, bearing a burden that nobody should ever be required to.

Then, on the most auspicious of days in the Bengali calendar, on Maha Ashtami, 1994, you took our leave. How, why, etc. etc. are questions which will forever seek to be answered. How do they really matter?

Many find it difficult to realize but you made a big difference to loads of people who were fortunate enough to connect with you. Who can forget the beggar with whom you shared lunch on the sidewalk, on a hot and dusty summer afternoon, in front of Garden Apartment? Or the people who benefited from your unbelievable charity that was as spontaneous as it was unlimited? The stories go on and on ....

Today, by the grace of the Almighty, your brothers have a more than reasonable life. However, the emptiness caused by your absence remains, whether we acknowledge it or not. Deep in our hearts, we continue to grieve that somewhere, somehow, we could not support our little brother as much as we could have, as we should have.

Before I sign off, just another point. Amongst us brothers, you were the only one who changed your name from Prasenjit

Ghosh to Prasenjit Maitra. **You alone had the mental strength to formally acknowledge the role played by Kaku in our lives after Baba left us.** While we were happy to bask in the sunlight of social recognition and the stability provided by Kaku, you were the only one who had the gumption to take this to its logical conclusion, to be adopted by him as his son, as his legal heir. Kaku may never have expressed it in so many words, but this made a huge difference to him, in a way that we failed to understand and appreciate.

Stay in peace, dear Baby. With Mamoni and Kaku, two people whose world began and ended with you, whose world revolved around you. God bless you, dear Baby, wherever you are. We love you. We miss you.

We wish that we could have done more for you. Much more ...

My wife, Aditi Ghosh (Koli)

What do you write, can you write, and what do you leave out when you try to recollect a journey, a partnership, a life spent together for twenty-seven years and counting? In the words of the immortal song from my favourite movie, Love Story,

Where do I begin, to tell the story of how great a love can be?

The sweet love story that is older than the sea

The simple truth about the love she brings to me

Where do I start?

Our journey together began on a Saturday in January 1995, when my parents took me along to her house, where she lived with her mother, sister, uncle, aunt and a cousin. Although it was a half-day at work, I still remember that I was held up in office and came home only around five p.m., tired and hungry.

Here we were, scheduled to be in Koli's house around five-thirty p.m. to meet my prospective bride and in-laws. As hard as I tried to wriggle out of the appointment, I could not. After hurriedly gulping down a late lunch, I found myself assessing and being assessed, if you know what I mean. As she put it to me some time later, I was distinctly uncomfortable and was sitting on the edge of the seat, desperately looking for a way out and at the earliest.

Once the initial period of unease was past us, and we had tucked in to delicious muffins, puff pastries and an invigorating cup of coffee, Koli and I started talking with each other, with me playing the role of a Gestapo interrogation officer. As some of you are aware, I had been through a brief but awfully difficult 'marriage' and an even more harrowing 'exit', if you can call it that, a couple of years back. I was acutely conscious of my depreciated value in the marriage market.

The first thing that I asked her was if she was fully aware of my not so glorious past and if so, why was she interested in taking things forward. More than appearance, family background and other factors that often play a determining role in arranged marriages, her response and my gut feeling about the genuineness of it were always going to be the deciding factors; at least in my mind.

Within a few minutes, it was clear that she strongly believed that the way forward was the only relevant way; that as long as the alignment of our minds and thoughts was in place, nothing else would and could matter. After that, it was all systems go.

On 18th February, 1995, we tied the knot and began our life together. Shortly thereafter, God blessed us with a little angel, Anushka and our cup of joy overflowed. This is not to say that we did not have a few bouts of teething trouble. They were mostly in the nature of turf wars that take place between the mother and the wife of the bridegroom, avoidable with a little patience and maturity. With time, these irritants, which appeared to be far more serious then, than what we realize them to be now, were smoothed over and life was good. God was smiling down on our family and we were blessed with an environment of love and affection.

A little less than five years down the road, we faced our first serious challenge. On 22nd December, 1999, I suffered a major heart attack while having my post-lunch cigarette (yes, I confess that I was a stupid young man who had picked up the deadly habit of lighting up about fifteen cancer sticks a day) and had to be rushed to hospital. While I did not know it then, my family was informed that it was a touch-and-go situation for the first couple of days, and this led me to being confined to my room at Woodlands Nursing Home for as long as seventeen days, no less. There were a few developments during this period that made me change my way of thinking quite drastically, which I have tried to cover elsewhere in this diary.

It would be churlish if I did not highlight a few aspects of our life together, which have significantly changed the lives of some of my most loved ones.

When we got married, and for a short while thereafter, as long as I was working with CESC, she had a flourishing career going. As an up-and-coming interior designer of Calcutta, she was known for her highly developed artistic sensibilities and attention to detail. Early on in her career, she had already received quite a bit of acclaim in the print media. She counted a number of corporate offices and industry barons amongst her clients. Things were promising, with the best yet to come.

However, two developments required us to take a close relook at our plans, and if necessary, some hard decisions. First, was the arrival of Anushka in our lives. Along with the joy and happiness, came parental responsibility. While being a good father meant providing for her, being a good mother was a different kettle of fish altogether. It meant giving up virtually every waking minute to your daughter, being with her when she was awake and taking care of daily chores when she was asleep.

The other event was my leaving CESC for Tata Consultancy Services (TCS). My CESC job was a nine-to-five job for five days a week and half a day on Saturdays, where the hours were predictable with few exceptions. Travel outside your base location was as infrequent as a blue moon, at least for me. Moving on to TCS, it was a completely different scene. Hours were long and unpredictable. A standing joke in IT (Information Technology) circles was that you knew when the working day starts, but not when it ends. Add to that frequent travels, national and international, sometimes for days, sometimes for a month at a stretch; you get the picture.

Between these two events, the call to be taken was simply this – would both of us continue to pursue our personal careers, with Chiki being brought up with the help of a nanny? Or would one of us step back, step away from the professional headlights, to make sure that Chiki would grow up in the loving shadow of a parent? Finally, if one of us had to take this huge backward step, who would it be?

The discussion around this critical issue, many thanks to Koli, was short and sweet. She was the one who raised her hand; she would be the one to nurture Chiki all the way from infancy to her dreams. Today, when we look at her, confidently marching forward to her destiny, **we thank God for making it possible and I look to Koli, for being His able conduit.**

There is another side of Koli, I need to bring out, on behalf of all three brothers. In August 2013, on the eve of the party we were hosting to mark Chiki's departure to USA and the beginning of her college education, Mamoni slipped and fractured her femur. At the advanced age of eighty-two, this usually means the end of any kind of mobility; for a person like Mamoni, it was a virtual death sentence. She needed to go through a hip-replacement surgery that went off quite well. A fall-out of this surgery, avoidable or not we will never know, was that her right leg was now slightly shorter than her left, and this made walking possible only with a support.

Back home, her recovery was slower than expected, even with the nurses who had been appointed to help the process. The main issue, we realized, was that the nurses had nobody to supervise them as well as they should be, with the result that they were becoming increasingly lax in their duties. Mamoni, by this time, was no longer the force she had always been, weakened by age and being by herself over the last few years, with her three sons in three different corners of the globe. Matters deteriorated to the point that she managed to develop bedsores and sciatica. We were all at our wits end, trying to figure out what was to be done.

At this critical juncture, Koli was the only person who was willing and able to take care of her in the way required, being by her side. She agreed to travel to Calcutta to be with her, to bring things back to normal or at least, as near normal could be. Over the next three years, from 2013 to 2016, Koli made multiple trips for months on end, tending to Mamoni in a way that forget any nurse, no daughter could ever do. Apart from taking care of her physically, from feeding to washing, she drove the fear of God into the nursing staff, shaking them out of their lethargy, mincing no words.

To make things complete, she also provided her with a huge portion of spiritual support by reading the Bible, playing CDs, explaining verses and in general, giving her hope. The environment at home became rejuvenated with liveliness replacing lifelessness, hope coming instead of despair and the fragrance of life replacing the stench of oncoming death and decay.

Things progressed to a point where Mamoni even resumed going to semi-urban and rural areas to provide medical consultation to people who would normally not have access to doctors of her stature. If age had not been totally against her, she would probably even have donned the surgeon's gown; I guess that even for her, it was now a bit too far to go. All in all, thanks to Koli's single-handed intervention in what was increasingly looking like a sinking ship, Mamoni regained her joy of living.

When Mamoni finally bid adieu to us, she did so with the fulfillment of a rewarding life well spent and well loved, in as dignified a manner as you could hope for. In no small measure, this was made possible by my darling wife, Koli. She made the transition from a daughter-in-law to a daughter and then went a fair distance further.

She added three years of high-quality time to Mamoni's life.

Life has now brought us to a point where, unimaginable as it might seem, the paths of Anushka will gradually diverge from the roads that Aditi and I will walk together. We need to avoid some of the errors made by our parents, mistaking over-protection and molly coddling for love and caring, not allowing our Gen-Next to carve out their destiny and make their life choices. While we will always be there, in flesh or spirit, supporting them as best as we can, we must not be smothering their individuality.

As Anushka says, ultimately it will be and must be Papa for Mama, and Mama for Papa. Koli and I have travelled a long road together, where there have been rainbows and dark clouds, bouts of rain and sunshine, portions of agony and ecstasy. Would I like to change it for any other? Absolutely not.

Together, we will walk into the sunset of our lives, off to the distant horizon.

My daughter, Anushka Ghosh (Chiki)

Chiki, Anushka, Ma Princesca Diamante

Shall I compare thee to a summer's day?

Thou art more lovely and more temperate

When you were born, during the first few days of your life, I must confess that I could handle you only with extreme trepidation. It was only after I was assured that your neck had strengthened adequately, did I dare to do the things I was looking forward to. Most of all, I loved to lie on my back, pick you up and move you, forwards and backwards.

On one such occasion, you decided that you had enough of these miniature airborne travels and decided to dump the contents of your stomach on mine, in small brown parcels. For a while, I did not realize what was happening, and then it struck me, figuratively and physically. I could not do much more than shout for Koli's help in what was clearly an emergency. She came in, gave me an amused smile, and then did the needful. Only on that day did I realize how awful it could feel to be bombed!

If ever there was a father, so impossibly in love with his daughter, it must be me. I know that there are many of us out there who feel exactly the same way. I like to believe that nobody could love their daughter as much as I do, and there could be no other girl who loves her father as much as Chiki does. Please note, whenever I ask her who she loves more, Chiki religiously responds 50-50. Not even a fraction of a percentage either way. Guess that she has been born with a diplomatic pouch!

Readers, please forgive me, but I am at a total loss for words. The purity of love, affection, consideration, empathy and joy that she has spread, wherever she goes, has to be seen to be understood. Later on, I will try to recount some of the episodes where she played starring roles, but she is much more than that. During times of strife or difficulty, she has always been an unwavering support, providing strength and sustenance to an extent that she had no business to provide, and that we had no business to ask for. And this, she has done time, after time, after time.

When we went to Bangalore for my bypass, I stayed at the hospital, being a patient. The others i.e. Mamoni, Mejda, Koli and Chiki, had rented an apartment close by. Every morning, at the crack of dawn, they would get up, do their morning business and rush to the hospital. Dinner would usually be a hastily prepared meal of rice, dal and fried potatoes. This routine continued for twelve long days; the only change being that on some days, the potato would be cut in long strips, while on others, it would be cut into circular discs. Mamoni was definitely not at her culinary best during this period; this meant that the food was as close to inedible as possible. To Chiki, it made no difference; she would always be the first to get ready, and cheer everybody's spirits by virtually marching all the way to the hospital and back.

On the day that I was undergoing the bypass surgery, what was Chiki doing? Was she sitting still in the corner, wondering along with everybody else how it would go? No, sir! She was leading all the young boys and girls there in the lobby, in prayer and walking around the hospital's deity, confident in the knowledge that He has the strength and the will to restore her father's good health, as well as the relatives of all the children who were gathered there, that day. Positive thinking in its best form, as Dr. Norman Vincent Peale would say.

Where does she get this inner strength, peace and tranquility? That makes her realize that 'this too shall pass', and that regardless of whatever, she will always be there by your side? Simply unbelievable.

I still fondly remember the days when I was recuperating after my surgery. Every day, she would come into the room and with utmost care not to cause any pain to me, cuddle up to my side and lie there, quietly. Even at the tender age of six, she understood the importance of just being there, where words are unnecessary.

Every day at lunch time, she would run to the pantry and ask for lunch to be served to patient no. 3 (that was me, of course). What was her interest? On the lunch plate, the only palatable item was the glass of fresh fruit juice. As soon as lunch was served and the serving lady was out of sight, Chiki would, without looking left or right, gulp it down. Then, she would invite me, with a twinkle in her eyes, to partake of the 'feast' comprising rice, sambhar, semi-boiled vegetables and curd. Which was absolutely unpalatable for any self-respecting Bengali. Guess that is why I lost nearly five kilograms over a period of two weeks, something that delighted my doctors.

In her own way, I suspect that this little angel was trying to lift my spirits by injecting a dose of mirth into the surroundings.

Another trait that I absolutely love about Chiki is her insatiable appetite to learn things, new and unrelated. For example, a favourite conversation of ours would be on differentiating between being smart and having good values. At other times, we would keep ourselves busy playing mental maths, solving puzzles and asking questions on general knowledge. She has this wonderful ability to switch from being frivolous to serious in a flash, recognizing the appropriateness of each. I guess that I could go on and on; it could really fill a book all by itself.

Darling Chiki, lest I be accused of painting a goody-goody uni-dimensional picture of you, let me make it clear that you are far from it. Let me recount a tale that is as hilarious, as it is insightful.

When you used to go to G.D. Birla by bus, at the ripe age of five, there was this other girl who used to go with you. Every day, there would be this unseemly scramble to see who would get on the bus earlier, with you coming out second best most of the times, as you used to give away quite a few kilograms and inches to your opponent.

Suddenly one morning, as the two of you were going through the expected tussle, the big school mate started running down the stairs, allowing you unhindered access to the bus. Koli could only stand there dazed, wondering what had happened. Later, when she asked you what had triggered the unexpected change in the other girl's behaviour, and that too so abruptly, you just smiled and with a deadpan face said "Mama, all I did was to tell her that attendants walk before the queen". That was enough. Beyond the naughtiness, it revealed a deep understanding of how human minds work, a realization that brawn can be neutralized by brains. God, how I love this facet of you. God bless you, dear child.

Triggered by how doctors gave your father a second lease of life, and inspired by Mamoni, you expressed your strong preference to pursue medicine as your career, if life did give you the necessary breaks. Today, you are studying medicine and by the grace of God, you will realize your dreams. You will, by His grace, also serve humanity and medical science as the years roll on.

This reminds me of your days in Warrington. You do know what I am referring to. Don't you? Day after day, you would come back after playing with friends, all messy and grimy. Koli would keep asking you how you managed to get muck all over your hands and face, but would not get any satisfactory answer.

Then came Borda, Boudi, Bumba and Bonnie. Naturally, they would join you and your friends in your fun and games. One day, Bumba came back crying, calling you cruel and what not. How could you be cruel? How could that be? It turned out that you and your friends had got into the habit of cultivating snails in glass jars full of plants. Once they were adequately fattened, you would practice your surgical skills on the unsuspecting snails. Enough to send Bumba to tears, but for you, this was just an aid to understanding the internals of a snail.

You are the shining light in our lives, and will be in all the lives that you will touch; be they in your family or in your professional life. You are indeed a special being, blessed by the Almighty to an extent that few have been. **Coupled with all your positive traits, your greatest strength has been your unshakeable faith and belief in Christ; may He continue to hold your hand strongly and be your guiding spirit forever.**

My sister-in-law, Mousumi Ghosh (Boudi)

With my marriage to 'the lady' being finalized, Borda came down, from Arnhem in early May 1991, to lend his weight and participate in the festivities. About four years back, Mamoni had gone to her beauty parlour and bumped into the wife of one of her sister's close friends, Meera Saha. While the beauticians kept on doing their stuff, these two ladies started chatting and what do you know? You guessed it! They discovered that there was this handsome young man, settled in Holland who was on the lookout for a 'suitable' (how I hate that word) lady to 'settle down with' (again, not a favourite phrase of mine).

As Borda was coming to attend my wedding, they reconnected on the subject. There was not too much time at hand, but for Mamoni, considerations such as shortage of time have never been a constraint. If she really wanted to get things done, the world could be moved around to make it happen. Within a couple of days, we landed up at Ranikuthi Government Housing Complex, which is where Boudi's family stayed.

We were five of us – Mamoni, Kaku and the brothers (except Mejda, who was still in Pune). After the pleasantries were done with, Boudi walked in, looking as graceful and elegant as she has always been. I am not sure if she knew who the prospective groom was, as there were three young men gazing at her, unblinkingly. I can imagine how unnerving this must have been for her; so what if she had been a teacher at a hotel management school.

Anyway, this uncertainty was soon cleared after the introductions were made, and now Borda and Boudi were free to openly ogle each other, size each other up and draw their own conclusions. Amidst nervous laughter and glances from the corners of their eyes, connections were established. Obviously, the life sciences concerned i.e., physics, chemistry and biology, worked well. As soon as we got into the car on the way home, Borda confessed, "Mamoni, I think that I am in love." We suspect that a similar declaration may have been made in Ranikuthi that evening, as well.

"The sooner good things progress, the better" so goes an old Indian saying. As there was not enough time for a social wedding to be organized, especially with the pomp and splendor planned for their younger daughter by the Saha family, it was decided that the marriage would be registered on 21st May, 1991 with the social wedding to follow on 6th August.

On the evening of the 21st, we went over to Boudi's place and the necessary formalities were gone through, followed by a hearty meal and plenty of fermented fruit juices, if you know what I mean. It was getting late, but nobody could be bothered. Suddenly, somebody rushed in and announced that the former Indian Prime Minister, Rajiv Gandhi, had been assassinated in an election rally. A nation-wide curfew had been imposed to avoid the kind of mindless violence that took place after the assassination of his mother, Prime Minister Indira Gandhi, seven years back. Abruptly, the evening came to an end and we went back home.

Early next morning, there was this newly married young man, Borda, sometimes sitting, sometimes pacing up and down the house listlessly. Mamoni, being perceptive, knew what was wrong, and what had to be done. She knew that her darling Igloo and her new Bouma, Chumki (Boudi's nickname) were pretty cut up and wanted to be with each other, not locked in each other's house.

The lovebirds just had to be brought together. So, what could be done?

She got into the car and zipped off to Ranikuthi. Earlier, she had called Boudi up and asked her to get ready and be dressed as if she was going to get admitted to a hospital. Although the curfew was on, doctors and ambulances were exempt, if they were transporting patients to and from a hospital. Taking advantage of this, she asked Boudi to lie down across the back seat and make suitable moans and groans, if they were stopped anywhere by curious onlookers. This ploy worked like a dream and within an hour, there was this lovey-dovey couple, grinning like Cheshire cats from ear to ear, super grateful to Mamoni for her spunk and quick thinking.

Boudi is now the proud mother of two absolutely wonderful children – a handsome boy, Sanjay (Bumba) and a darling girl, Natasha (Bonnie). Both of them are charting out their lives in exciting frontiers and we eagerly wait to see where it takes them. While Bumba is a couple of years older than Chiki, Bonnie is two years younger. It would be great if, over the years, they can bond well amongst themselves and form a truly powerful group of three.

Sanjay was born on the auspicious day of Mahalaya and can be described as the "wise man with dreams". I have been told of the day he came back from his first day at school and asked his mother "Mama, why don't we speak human language at home"? That's when she realised, that it must be quite confusing for a child to be out there in a Dutch world, and then come back to a little India at home. She decided to integrate herself even more into the Dutch way of living! He has always been a kind hearted thinker and an avid reader, with a steadfast hunger for knowledge, be it history, geography, science, politics, art! In many ways he reminds me of me, if I may be allowed to say so.

After finishing Gymnasium Secondary School, he earned his Bachelor's degree in International Business and Masters in Strategic Innovation Management. When looking for a job, he wanted to make a difference to society as well as have time to pursue his hobbies of writing short stories and poems, of climbing and deep sea diving. Hence, he refused to get into the corporate world and chose a job with the Government of the Netherlands as a smart energy advisor. It's his dream to be able to open his own diving school someday.

Natasha came into the world with a struggle, 4 years after her brother. And she is a fighter, a coconut-hard shell with a soft centre! They say morning shows the day. And that is so true for Natasha. As a baby, she would not eat unless there was music playing in the background, her favourite song being 'Nothing Else Matters' by Metallica. In fact, she could count backwards from 40 much before she could actually count – this is because she used to listen to the Top 40 on radio as a baby! And her passion for music remains, and grows till date.

If there is anything one can learn from Natasha, it's perseverance. With her hard work and never say die spirit, she finished the challenging Gymnasium school with flying colours, while working on her music on the side. She has grown up to be a very caring person with a lot of determination. Today, after completing her Master in Business Organisation and Policy, she is working as a Campaign Manager with a start-up company, while music remains her passion. She has mastered the ukulele and is a singer and songwriter with thousands of followers worldwide. It's her dream to take her own music company to soaring heights.

I have not been able to spend a lot of time with Boudi, for she has been with Borda in Holland throughout. Based on the limited interaction that I have had with her, I can, in all honesty, say that even if I had a few more Boudis, she would definitely be my favourite. **Responsible, supportive, loving and erudite; these attributes apply in good measure to** her. She also happens to be an accomplished cook. With her culinary expertise extending across a wide range of cuisines, could it be any different? She is also fond of Scrabble, a popular word-making game, something that is a common passion for both Koli and I.

The stories I have heard from Mejda who has spent far more time with her, in Pune, Arnhem and Calcutta, only reaffirm my thoughts about her. I can only hope that in the years ahead, we can spend some serious good quality time with each other, God in His infinite grace, allowing that to happen.

My cousin, Chandreyi Banerjee (Tani)

The time I have spent with Tani can broadly be split into two periods; between 1969 and 1972, and from 1972 onwards. These two periods were as different as possible, as chalk is from cheese.

The first period started in February 1969, when we came to New Alipur late at night after a four-day long drive all the way from Digboi, after our family had been splintered by events of the recent past. Once we had regained our bearing and life a semblance of stability, we became part of a joint family comprising my grandparents, father, three brothers, my uncle's family and our unmarried aunt (Pipi).

Chandreyi (Tani) is three months older than me, while Indrani (Tunu) is six years younger. Their youngest sister, Sujata (Munmun) was born in July 1973, but that was after Baby and I had moved to Hyderabad. Therefore, our interaction with her has been much less than with Tani or Tunu.

Soon, we were admitted to Calcutta Boys School, which was close to Tani's school, Loreto Day School. Due to the proximity of the schools and their timings, Mejda, Tani and I would go and come back from school together. This was the first angle of a multi-faceted relationship that would develop over the years.

Next, having no friends to speak of when we suddenly landed in New Alipur, Tani's friends gradually became my friends, with some of them continuing to be so until this day, most notably Apu and Panku. If I developed a fair level of expertise in girlie games e.g. hop scotch and dark room; herein lay the genesis of these proclivities. It also explains why I never got actively involved in typical boy sports such as cricket and football; after all, my friends just did not play those games.

However, the strongest tie between Tani and me had nothing to do with friends, fun and games. It was rooted in just a harsh fact of life, extreme deprivation. If one had to do justice to the limitations we faced, it would probably fill more than a few chapters. For the sake of brevity, I will give only a flavour of how things were.

We were always on the tightest possible budget that there could be. For going to and from school, only the exact bus fare would be handed over to us; the way to get any spare money was if we managed to evade the bus conductor during the whole ride. To those who would like to talk of honesty and values, we dare them to live the life we lived, when we were pre-pubescent children with growing appetites. Mind you, we had already tasted the goodies of life and acquired a hunger for the same.

Sunday lunch was special for us, not because our larger family would get together, but because it would elevate our meal from rice, dal, a vegetable curry and a miniscule piece of fish to rice and mutton curry. Tani and I still recall, in details, a particular Sunday lunch where we challenged ourselves to see how many chapattis we could have. One, two, three ... we went all the way up to nine. That tells you how hungry we would normally be, what a growing appetite is. Oh! I forgot to mention how much mutton we ate with the nine decent sized chapattis; just two not large pieces. I clearly remember that we ate the first eight chapattis with only gravy and potatoes, preserving the mutton for a grand ending to our feast.

Going beyond deprivation, was the discovery of various aspects of life, that ranged from stumbling across her father's stack of Playboy magazines to being at the wrong end of differential treatment (I am talking of little boys and girls, not adults regarding whom you could have a host of issues). This stretched to the point that the nursery school teacher remarked to Mamoni how strange it was that qualitatively different tiffin boxes would come for different children, from the same house. Oh! The list can go on and on. It is no surprise that having been witness to, and being victims of, a traumatic childhood, **both of us have done everything possible to shield our children from anything like this in their lives.**

Beyond 1972, both of us have faced challenges in life, with the difference being that time had made us stronger. We have been able to face life with a far greater degree of assurance, supported by our family members. In this respect, I must confess that I have been more fortunate than Tani. Maybe, this led her to make certain choices that have been more difficult. All in all, life has not been easy or smooth for us, especially during our formative years. Both of us bear scars that have stubbornly refused to go away; regardless of how well we try to camouflage them or time tries to lighten them.

My youngest aunt, Shukla Majumdar (Pipi)

If I had to identify the finest person there could be, and yet the person who was just bypassed by Fate, in a manner of speaking, that person had to be only you, dear Pipi.

A late comer to the KC Ghosh family, you were just about six years older than Borda and Mejda, who were more your friends than nephews. Baba was a father figure to you, being twenty-three years older, and this was reflected in the extreme respect that you always had for him. When you were just a teenager, we left for Digboi and I did not get to know you till we came back to Calcutta in February 1969, emotionally wrecked after the break-up of our parent's marriage.

My earliest memories of you are of this tall and strong lady, who brooked no competition in the women's races and could have given many of the boys a run for their money. On the other hand, you were this absolutely adorable aunt of mine, who would get me ready for school, mash the rice, dal and potatoes before lovingly feeding it to me as we rushed to get to the bus stop in time.

With Borda and Mejda, you were their closest friend and confidante, along with your dear friend, Boni. I still remember the mumbo-jumbo language (adding an extra 'n' sound after every syllable) you had developed, to be able to speak freely in front of others, without anybody catching on to what you were talking about. I also remember your fondness for Bharati aunty, Purna aunty, Indira aunty and others, who you loved to visit as often as you could. For those wondering where did all these aunties come from, let me give you a clue; three of the most popular movie theatres in South Calcutta were Indira, Purna and Bharati. Later on, you moved to Government Art College where you developed your circle of friends, many of whom turned out to be distinguished in the fields of arts and crafts, market research etc.

In May 1970, you married Supriyo Majumdar (Chhoto Khokon Kaku), and moved, ten minutes walking distance, to your in-law's place. I still remember how Thamma would tell me that now that 674 was your in-law's house, I should reduce the frequency of my visits there, where I used to love going to chat with Bunu Pipi, your sister-in-law.

With you leaving our house, 735 definitely lost a lot of its charm.

Shortly thereafter, Baba passed away, and we moved to Hyderabad. We would come, once a year, to spend our summer holidays at 735. I remember the first time we came, in April 1973, there was this absolutely beautiful little angel in your lap, our darling Bubu (Suchandra). Oh, what a thrill it was to push her around in the pram, feeling protective and responsible. Bubu grew up to be your most favourite girl, (Monai, don't be upset), and in her every act, every dress, every dream, you relived your own days gone by. That's what I felt, and I don't think that I am off the mark.

The next time we came, there you were with a large tummy, and poor little I was asked not to sit on your lap, as I loved to. I remember that you had this guilty look on your face, as if you were apologetic for getting in the family way.

The young girl who arrived, on 5th October, 1974, was a special child. At the time of her birth, Monai (Suparna) did face a few health issues. Consequently, she had additional nutritional requirements. God alone knows how you managed to maintain her health as well as you did, not the least with endless glasses of pomegranate juice, vegetables and all that the doctor prescribed, or even suggested.

Somebody with a lesser sense of determination and stamina would have accepted the dictates of fate, but you, dear Pipi, were made of a different mettle altogether. Today, if Monai is a healthy lady of forty-seven, more than fulfilling her responsibilities as a dutiful daughter and loving mother as she is, a big chunk of this is due to you, dear Pipi. For her, you have been much more than a mother.

Coming to the equation we brothers had with you, it has always been the most wonderful side of our life in New Alipur. The sheer love and affection in your voice and face, visible whenever we dropped into your house, regardless of your other pre-occupations, was always as spontaneous as it could be.

On the special occasion of Bhai phota (when sisters apply sandalwood paste on the forehead of their brothers, praying for their long life and seeking their protection), the traditional breakfast of luchi, aloo-phulkopir chhenchki, chholar dal and mishti would never taste the same, if it wasn't in your house, lovingly served by you.

Out of nowhere, the big bad C struck you in early 2004. Khokon Kaku fought with all his might to keep this monster at bay, and you tried to help the fight by staying as positive and brave as you could, but in front of our disbelieving eyes you slipped away to the arms of the Almighty in July 2004. A particularly sad part of this, for me, was that I had to leave Calcutta just before you said goodbye; I could not even be there on your final journey.

By the grace of God, Borda and Mejda, who along with Tani were probably your three closest friends, were there to hold your hand as your loving eyes closed for eternity.

Those whom the gods love, go back to his arms soon. Pipi, you are proof of this. **You left far too early, but I guess that the gods could not bear your absence any longer.**

My inspirational friend, Suki

On a damp afternoon, in early 1974, we moved from our house in Somajiguda to the most wonderful place that we have ever stayed in, nestled in the rocky terrains of Banjara Hills. This place was a set of four double-storied bungalows located on a hilltop, in a place called College Park, as it was the property of Administrative Staff College of India (ASCI).

Leading up to the top, there was a long winding road from the main gate. To add to the romantic charm of the place, this road went under an old stone brick bridge, heavily covered with shrubs and weeds, infested with snakes and other lovable creatures. Towards the end of the road, it led into an open area that had two vertical brick walls, being the ruins of old buildings. All in all, it was a place to absolutely captivate your mind and difficult to describe, if you have not seen it.

To return to the narrative, on the day we moved in to House No. 3, College Park the other families had arranged an open-air lunch to welcome us. This was a nice gesture indeed, totally in keeping with the culture of ASCI and the spirit of Hyderabad. While the food and drinks were being passed around, and people were engaged in friendly chit chat, I noticed a little eight-year-old girl. She was quietly sitting there, staying away from the food (she had a stomach upset), just soaking in the moment and figuring out the newcomers.

This young lady, dear friend, was Suki. Over the years, she became one of my dearest friends and in many ways, my inspirational friend, even though she was six years my junior. I have jotted some of my most vivid memories about her elsewhere in this memoir, but suffice to say that I could fill an entire book on her alone, without being able to do full justice to her. **God bless her, and all around her, for there are not too many people who can hold a torch to her.**

She is special, truly extra special.

Sandy Aunty

Apart from being the mother of my dearest friend, she was the one closest to Mamoni, during their years together in College Park. She also happens to be somebody I felt a strong bonding with, and still continue to do, regardless of how long we have not interacted with each other. Today, I can confidently turn up at her door step and start chatting with her as if we were just picking up the strings from yesterday, even if ten years or more have gone by.

Sandy Aunty is a 2nd generation immigrant from Syria to USA. In college, she was a beauty queen, and I have seen quite a few newspaper clippings that bear testimony to the head turning charm and beauty that she had. It was too much for BL uncle, a brilliant Ph.D. student from Rajasthan, India to resist. Rather quickly, she hitched her wagon and soon became a proud mother to Suki, before moving to the academic environs of ASCI, to the lovely commune called College Park. Shortly after coming to India, she got God's gift of a darling boy, Vijai, in 1969.

As my most vivid memories of Suki and Vijai relate to the period 1974 to 1978, when we used to stay in College Park, I still struggle to think of them as the people they have both grown up to be, two wonderfully mature and special persons.

The first thing that comes to mind, when I think of Sandy Aunty, is the atmosphere of openness that she cultivated, so effortlessly, in her home. No pretense, no showmanship, nothing that was anything but what things actually were. You were free to join in for lunch or dinner unannounced; at least I used to do it so often; and never be apologetic if the fare on the table was simple and wholesome, without being fancy. She was happy to offer whatever was available, be it pan cakes, scones and jam, or dal, roti and cabbage sabji. It made no difference to her, and she expected all at the table to understand likewise. Food was something that needed to be had to fill our stomachs and provide nutrition, not make any pointless statements.

The other fascinating aspect was that nothing was taboo in her discussions with her children, not even in the presence of outsiders. As mentioned, I would frequently join in at meals, but it altered not her openness in any way.

I remember this occasion when their maid servant was visibly pregnant, but she did not have her husband with her. There was talk, the hush-hush variety, that she was involved with the gardener but there was no confirmation to be had. I was sitting at the dining table, just about to pop the roti with dal and gobi sabji into my mouth, when Vijai suddenly looked at Sandy Aunty, and asked:

"Mummy, who put the baby in Laxmi's (the maid in question) tummy? Was it the gardener?" (As events subsequently turned out, Vijai was totally on the spot; it was indeed the gardener who was the father of Laxmi's baby. There is a lot to be said for child-like intuition!)

I came close, very close, to choking and ejecting the morsel from my mouth, for more than one reason. First, here was this seven-year-old boy asking his mother about the processes of life and birth, without any hesitation, at all. Secondly, his question implied a greater degree of understanding of reproductive processes than most children who were quite a few years older. And finally, this conversation was taking place, in front of an outsider. Was nothing off the table?

To my utter consternation, what happened next was even more eye-opening. Sandy Aunty proceeded to have a rather mature and adult conversation on the subject, with Vijai and Suki nodding their heads sagely, absorbing what was on offer.

That particular meal taught me a lesson that has shaped me hugely over the years, and has encouraged me to be free and frank, no matter what. Koli and I have done our best to nurture a similar openness in our dealings with Chiki, as well as with others who do not get intimidated by this attitude of ours.

Pipi's sister-in-law, Sutapa Majumdar (Bunu Pipi)

Sutapa Majumdar, or Bunu Pipi as she is affectionately called by me. One of my favourite persons with whom I have always had a wonderful relationship, something that a lot of people have struggled to come to terms with, both in her family and mine. She is the younger sister-in-law of somebody else who was dear to me, my dear adorable Pipi.

Shortly after we moved from Digboi to Calcutta, during those horrible days, Bunu Pipi was one person who brought smiles to my face, who understood the turmoil in my heart and gave me solace through her collection of books and endless discussions.

Day after day, I remember walking down from our house to hers, after finishing my homework. Invariably, she would be waiting on the verandah looking out to the roads, watching life pass by. She would greet me warmly and we would start chatting on whatever subject took our fancy. Discussion topics varied across a wide spectrum, but whatever they were, these sessions helped in two ways. Not only would they take my mind away from the omnipresent pain and misery that seemed to surround me everywhere, it also opened my minds to horizons that most around me were, frankly, incapable of, or just not interested in. From Ben Hur to World War II, from distant lands to oceanic marvels, we covered it all.

Later on, I got to visit her in Hyderabad many times. Each and every time, the warmth and affection that was evident in the way she reached out to me, only reaffirmed my belief that here was someone who was more than just a relative by marriage. Here was a true friend of mine.

I still remember the first time I went to her home in Hyderabad; all that I had to go on was her husband's name, the organisation he worked in and the name of the locality (that had, I would guess about 10,000 houses). Armed with only this limited information, I somehow managed to reach her place. Bunu Pipi was as astounded at this as I was, but I guess if God so wills it, and if you want something badly enough, the entire universe strives to make it happen for you (*Apologies, to Farah Khan for transcribing the theme from her film, Om Shanti Om*).

Over the years, as this deep friendship, bond if I may call it, strengthened between Bunu Pipi and me, I know that a lot of people found it strange. What kind of relationship could possibly exist between a nineteen-year-old lady and a boy of ten, who were not related in anyway, except through marriage between their families? What could be the common bond that both of them found so wonderful that it only grew stronger with the passage of time? Ask me these questions, and I will not be able to provide any coherent answers. All I know is that whenever I am around Bunu Pipi, I feel a sense of comfort, a strange sense of being able to relate to somebody that I have not been able to with many others 'closer' to me.

(*Shades of Rishi Kapoor, in "Mera Naam Joker", the adolescent boy who developed an adorable crush on his class teacher, Simi? Hmmm ... now that could be something worth thinking about ... Not entirely laughable, to be honest*)

I have often heard the phrase – **Friends are relatives you choose to have.** Bunu Pipi, surely, you are one. By a strange coincidence, Sutapa also happened to be the name of another dear friend of mine, Sutapa Roy (Pinky), who I will try to do justice to elsewhere in my journey down memory lane. Wonder what it is that makes the Sutapa-s of the world special, at least as far as I am concerned ...My younger cousin, Indrani Tollan (Tunu)

The rebel without a cause, James Dean. The rebel with a cause, Indrani Tollan, Tunu. The cause? No mediocrity, please!

From as early as I can remember, Tunu was different, in every way possible. As a young girl, she could take down with ease, boys considerably older and bigger than her. In fact, I remember that when she was about eight, she and Baby (who was a couple of years older) were playing the fool with each other. Suddenly, Baby, in a fit of exasperation, just reached out and pulled her panties down. How did she react? Did she cry in shame, or run to her mother for help? Definitely not. She just caught Baby's lower leg and wrenched it so hard, so very hard, that he writhed in pain; not just for the day but for weeks thereafter. His knee had been dislocated. This was the essence of spirit, a la Tunu.

In high school, she was a spirited fun-loving girl, living the full life with its fair share of the good and the not so good, the bold and the beautiful. She appeared to be quite casual about her academics, as if it did not really matter to her. On the day the results of her Board exams were announced, everybody at home was quite concerned; would she pass or would she not? Come the evening of results day, Tunu slowly trudged back home, not looking skywards at all. People rushed forward to console her, telling her there was always a second chance, not to get so despondent, patting her on the back comfortingly.

At this point, she looked up, and the reason for her continued downward stare became clear to all. She was giggling away silently, trying her best not to make a sound, for wonder of wonders, not only had she passed the exam, she had aced it. She had done so earning a First Division. This was no mean feat, something that few in our family had achieved. Everybody was stunned into silence. This was Tunu, the silent champ, who just loved to play pranks, when you least expected her to. Some of the pranks played by her are absolutely unforgettable, both in their conception and execution, but I will go into them some other time.

Around the late eighties, she came across a Cathay Pacific advertisement, for air hostesses. Not bothering about eligibility criteria and such minor technical details, she put in her application with nobody at home being any the wiser. Stage by stage, she kept clearing the selection processes, with only a couple of her closest friends having any clue of what was going on. One fine day, when she got the final appointment letter and the initial posting order, she broke the news at home, and once again, everyone was completely taken aback. True to her character, **she had embarked on this journey all by herself, without anybody's support and relying on nobody's advice, knowing that she would have to chart her own destiny**, if she was not to get stuck in the quagmire of mediocrity.

In 1994, she married her sweetheart, a young lawyer who was on military duty in Hong Kong, Richard Tollan. They are now the proud parents of two handsome young men, William and Matthew. Like any couple, they have had their ups and downs, but that is only to be expected when people come from such diverse backgrounds. Their love for each other has always been strong enough to weather any challenge.

From being the high-spirited, full of pranks teenager to the caring mother of two boys and a loving wife, to an elegant lady who runs her gorgeous household in a picture-perfect manner, Tunu fits the tag line of Virginia Slims better than anybody I know "You have come a long way, lady."

Mediocrity is a word that you have always shunned in your life. Anything but the best has never been good enough for you. Long may you stay the way you are, dear Tunu.

The queen bee – Indrani Chakravorty (Rumni)

Leading the group of young ladies in our class at JU, in every way possible, was this elegant lady who had a penchant for always being in formal attire. Nothing other than crisply starched, fresh out of the laundry pastel-coloured sarees, often with striking geometric patterns, would do. Along with that, she would have her matching hand bag and there, you see her perfectly dressed, always cool and composed, ready to conquer the world with effortless ease.

She mixed with all and sundry with élan, with friendliness and grace. However, if anybody ever deigned to cross the boundary of friendliness into over-friendliness, or even attempted to crack jokes that were not entirely appropriate, she was quick to cut them down with a scything look. Time may have dimmed some of the particulars, but you do get the general picture.

Having joined JU only towards the middle of the 2nd year, just a few months before the Part One exams, I needed to catch up with the study material covered till then. Here, it will be amiss if I did not mention the tremendous help that I got from Indrani, and another girl in our class, Indu, a Tamilian Brahmin. I will jot down my memories covering Indu elsewhere. Without the extensive and clear notes that I got from the two of them, catching up with the rest of the class would have been but a pipe dream. An incidental benefit was that this also provided a communication bridge with the two of them, as it was more than a little difficult to reach out to them otherwise. Two birds with one stone, eh?

Here, I would like to mention a side of her that marked her out to be somebody special, somebody different from the rest of us. She was always, and by that, I mean always with no exceptions, the perfect hostess to a degree that would often leave us open-mouthed. Apart from the food being delicious beyond compare, each item being perfectly coordinated with every other, the table was laid out with extreme care; the cushions arranged in geometric precision; the list goes on and on.

To complete the picture of being the perfect hostess, she would also make the arrangements for card games and have discussion topics ready that appealed to our likes. Every time we went to her house, we would come away with the feeling that time had passed too quickly and wondering when we could do it again.

Based on our limited exchanges over the first few days, and from what I heard about her from others, it became clear that apart from her external grace and poise, she was an exceptional student. If you harboured any hopes of landing the big prize at the end of the graduating class, she was, quite clearly, the one to beat. To be honest, while getting to know girls and all that was something that we naughty boys looked forward to, I had another serious mission of sorts to fulfill.

In the light of Kaku's words, so clearly articulated when I was deciding between science and economics on the way forward, I had a burning desire to get that elusive gold medal from the Vice Chancellor of JU, at the graduation ceremony for our class, come what may. Right in front of me, between me and the shining medal, stood the elegant and classy lady,

Indrani Chakravorty. Although the proverbial gauntlet was not thrown down, it was all too clear that this was a truly formidable adversary who I had to overcome, if I had any hopes of realizing my dreams. Gradually, she became one of my dearest friends, but that is another.

Before I sign off, let me bring up something that I have sometimes alluded to, during our conversations with close friends. Shortly before the Part Two exams, based on which the final grades would be determined, her mother needed to undergo a major surgery. Apart from all the worries that come along with a major surgical procedure, was the absolutely horrible timing, in so far as she was concerned.

It was scheduled for just a couple of months before our Part Two exams. Add to that, the post-surgery stay in the hospital and the convalescence care thereafter; this was bound to take a huge toll on her preparation time, she being the only other lady in her house. Every day, after college, as we did not have the system of study leave those days, she would go home, cook dinner for the family and then carry the home-cooked food to the hospital to feed her mother. Thereafter, she would come back home and prepare for the next day. Preparatory studies for the most important examinations of her life were pushed way back in the list of priorities. This was clear to us in class, not the least in her exhausted eyes and demeanor.

At this critical juncture before the exams, a make-or-break point, something within me cried out "You think that you are honourable, that you like a fair fight. Are you willing to walk the talk?" It was not an easy call to make. However, the urge to stand tall in my own eyes, regardless of tactical considerations, made me take a decision that I am proud of, and will remain so, till my dying day. I decided not to touch my books after college hours, as long as her mother was in the hospital. In my own humble way, I was trying to create a level playing field.

As things finally played out, she did, deservedly, take away the yellow medal. In all honesty, never did I regret my decision to go with the call for honour, over a possible shot at what could or may have been. This remains a prize that nobody can take away from me, a laurel that I cherish and will do, for life.

Often, I used to call her as Mokkhi Rani, or Queen Bee. Why? Simply because she stood out as being a unique combination of propriety without being snooty. She was the picture of grace and friendliness without encouraging, leave alone tolerating, extra-familiarity. Always elegant and able to shoulder responsibility, whenever called upon to do so – that was Indrani.

A friendship born out of fierce competition, but fought in the healthiest and most respectful of manners. **A friendship strengthened by honour and a strong sense of fair play, nurtured by shared values**. It has lasted for more than four decades. That's how I would like to describe my friendship with you, dear Indrani.

A dear friend, down the ages – Shubhra Sapru (Mithu)

I landed in Jadavpur University in mid-1978, in a co-educational class for only the second time in my life (I had spent the previous year at Nizam College, Hyderabad which was also a co-educational institution). It would have been far more awkward and difficult, from every angle that you can imagine, if it had not been for two girls in particular, Arunima (Miti) and Shubhra (Mithu). What made it even easier for me was the fact that these girls lived in Dover Lane, close to where I used to stay in Mandeville Gardens, just a stone's throw away.

Right from the beginning, the three of us formed a group that was as closely knit as could be. A strong glue that bound us together was our common background of being what is called 'probashi bangali' or non-resident Bengalis. This was reflected in our lack of comfort with the richness of Bengali literature, culture and traditions.

There was something else that strengthened our ties. It was our practice of common studies, in a rather interesting manner. In class, Miti and Mithu would take down notes, as copiously as they could, while I would concentrate fully on the actual lecture itself. After classes, we would go over to the residential complex where these girls lived, and I would take the notes from them and explain what was taught in class. This worked well for us; I strongly recommend this method for group studies.

After graduation, while many of us went our own separate ways to destinations far and near, Mithu and I continued to stay in close touch with each other. This was in spite of the fact that she went off to Sierra Leone and then to London, before coming down to settle in Bombay. On my part, I managed to spend some time in UK and am now in Saudi Arabia for the last twelve years. Regardless of distances and time zones, we have stayed connected to a degree where we can just pick up the phone, punch out the other's phone number and our conversation picks up from exactly where we left off, in a manner of speaking.

I still remember, oh so very clearly, how disoriented I became when Mithu had to leave Calcutta, with a very short notice, to Sierra Leone and London, as her father got a plum UNIDO posting in Freetown (incidentally, Indu was the only person in our group who had even the slightest clue where that was – "Isn't' Sierra Leone on the Western bulge of Africa?" – Mithu confessed that she could have jumped up in joy and given Indu the tightest possible hug, right then and there). Life just wasn't the same, and for the first time for as long as I can remember, I actually got into the habit of writing letters and waiting eagerly for her response – in her nearly flat, straight line but clear handwriting. Something was definitely missing – yes, my dear friend was being missed badly!

There have been occasions when I have had but a few hours in Bombay, but that has been enough for me to go over to her place, with virtually no prior intimation, and there would she be, serving up a hot and delicious lunch of Kashmiri fish curry or rogan josh. Or if I had just an evening in Bombay, to hop over to their place and go along with Siddharth (her handsome Kashmiri Brahmin husband) and Sumati (her lovable daughter) for a Gujarati thali meal at Rajbhog.

When we were trying to relocate to Saudi Arabia, we stayed in Mithu's house more than once, without the slightest hesitation on our part and I think, without the least amount of irritation on hers, although we would have caused a fair degree of inconvenience. Such has been the comfort and confidence in our relationship.

Our friendship has flowered to a degree that we really have few secrets from each other. Your joy is mine, my pain is yours, to paraphrase the words of a popular Hindi song; this describes our relationship quite aptly, I believe.

Our friendship continues to blossom and grow stronger by the day.

A sweet girl caught between cultures – Indu

Indu was, far and away, the sweetest and most innocent flower that bloomed in our Economics Department, JU. When I think of her, I can't help but hum the lines from the song "I am sixteen" from the musical, The Sound of Music, which goes as follows:

I am sixteen, going on seventeen, I know that I'm naïve

Fellows I meet may tell me I'm sweet and willingly, I believe

I am sixteen, going on seventeen, innocent as a rose

Bachelor dandies, drinkers of brandies, what do I know of those

Totally unprepared am I, to face a world of men

Timid and shy, and scared am I, of things beyond my ken

When I came to JU for the first time, I was desperately in need of class notes as I had joined in the middle of the second year. Indu, as she was affectionately called, was kind enough to lend me her notes, written in her clear and pearly handwriting that was a pleasure to read. We became quite thick, being part of a close group that would always be hanging out together.

In her, I saw a girl who was a little lost and bemused, being a Tamilian Brahmin in the heart of Calcutta, being a hard-core vegetarian in a group that devoured anything that walked, flew or swam and most importantly, being part of a mixed gender group, never having done so in her life. Naturally, she clung to a handful of girls for support, to help her avoid any of the pitfalls that may lie in wait for her. In addition, rightly or wrongly, she felt somewhat discriminated against, because of her lack of fluency in Bengali and being marked as an outsider.

I suppose that was a major reason why she used to hang out with our group, as many of us had spent a considerable amount of time outside West Bengal. College being college, and teenagers being what they are, she faced her fair share of leg pulling by our classmates, all in perfectly good humour and taste. Most of us were well aware of the conservative upbringing that she had come from, and took care to avoid offending her sensibilities, but once in a while, we just may have.

When the final results came out, Indu was more than a little disappointed with her performance and went into a shell of sorts. This was unfortunate, as shortly thereafter, she left Calcutta for her hometown. She is now happily settled in USA, along with her son, who is a brilliant doctor, and her daughter, who is a practicing lawyer and is now happily married.

God bless her with peace and bliss along life's journey. **She will always remain in my heart as an innocent, pure and sensitive soul, who could do no harm to those around her and always had the highest sense of values and ethics.**

A whiff of fresh air – Krishnakali Mazumder (Krishna)

Krishnakali, or Krishna as we knew her in our college days. Always the beautiful, smiling young lady in our class, usually accompanied by at least one of her two friends – Urmila Bhattacharya in JU or Sharmila Maitra outside it. She is one of those few ladies that nature forgot to consider in its ageing process. Four decades have gone by since we exited the hallowed portals of our university; Krishna looks, sounds and behaves today just the same as she did back then.

Like moths are attracted to a flame, like bees to a flower, so were the guys in JU to this lady beautiful. Unfortunately for some of us, this list included even boys from other faculties, especially those from the Chemical Engineering stream in our university. Absolutely unfair, for how could Arts faculty students compete with the high and mighty products of engineering colleges? One of these days, a law should be enacted to prevent such 'hijackings', as it is clearly a game between unequals.

Jokes apart, Krishna has always been one of the most pleasant persons that you could hope to have around you.

Always game for a laugh, always ready to join into a picnic or a day at the movies, she was surprisingly serious in respect of her academics too. This aspect I discovered much later, in fact, two years after I had passed out of JU. After completing my MBA, I was required to learn computer programming in COBOL, for which I joined a six-week course at Regional Computer Centre. Surprise, surprise, who do I see joining me in the course? It was none other than Krishna.

At first, I thought that this was just a TPA (Time Pass Activity) for her, but I quickly realized that it definitely was not. She was one of the most serious students in the class, far more than many of the others (read guys) in our course, giving a big rebuttal to the much-touted gender divide; boys are serious, while girls come to grab the boys' eye balls. Another myth went out of the window. If I remember correctly, she was near the top of the class, when the final certificates were handed out.

Getting married in May 1985, (yes, you guessed it, to one of those engineering graduates) she has been blessed with a handsome boy and a beautiful girl both of whom have entered the matrimonial world recently. For as long as I can remember, whenever she comes to Calcutta, we make it a point to have some seriously good times together, either as two families or as two dear friends. We have been together a long time, through times good and not so good. I remember, with particular relish, the fun-filled New Year parties that we have had on our rooftop flat in Jodhpur Park. It was during one of these parties Chiki made her unforgettable observation "Why did Krishna Aunty have to wish you Happy New Year and give you a hug every time, five times?" I came close to giving her a spank, not for exaggerating but for having nothing better to do than keep count.

Krishna has always been a dear friend of mine, and I look forward to our friendship staying vibrant and warm, as it has always been.

Siblings of another mother – Munjal and Kaajal Mehta

To call Munjal and Kaajal my friends is like calling the Pacific Ocean a body of water. Factually correct, but contextually, absolutely incomplete.

Munjal first came into our lives, or to be more precise, into Mejda's life in the early eighties, when both of them joined Asiatic Oxygen; one as a fresh chemical engineer from National Institute of Technology, Durgapur, the other as a gold medalist from Indian Institute of Planning & Management, New Delhi. One determined to gain technological mastery over gases and cryogenics, while the other was looking to create and capture markets. And, if I may say so, a Laurel and Hardy. Munjal, please don't kill me with your deadly stares.

After a brief period of learning the game in the corporate world, these two, along with the technical lead of Asiatic Oxygen, Mr. Aditya, decided that it was time for them to venture into the world of gas manufacturing and cryogenic vessels on their own. They were primarily driven by enthusiasm and relied rather heavily on Mr. Aditya, as he was the man with the domain knowledge, industry contacts and most importantly, the experience that was critical for a venture of this nature.

For some reason that is not clear to me, Mejda and Munjal put in their papers before Mr. Aditya and got going in their brave new entrepreneurial world, perched atop their chariot, Shell-N-Tube. In time, they procured their first order, to repair an oxygen storage tank in Guwahati, Assam.

Out of nowhere, Mr. Aditya suddenly announced that he had reconsidered his decision to resign and hence, would not be a part of Shell-N-Tube. Munjal and Mejda were now out on a limb, facing a truly Hobson's choice. They could either eat humble pie and crawl back to Asiatic Oxygen with the tail between their legs, or could continue forward into the big bad world of business, having neither capital nor experience, having neither contacts nor track record. All they had was confidence in their ability and faith in the Almighty.

They decided not to take a backward step, and I am proud to state that they have never, not once in the four decades that they have spent together, done so. Going forward was the only option; while the ground reality was that they now had an order to execute but not the money to buy even their tickets to go to the plant site.

It was at this point of time, that both of them came to my office, requesting for a small loan to help tide over this period. The amount requested was Rs. 2,000, nothing more. Granted that this was not exactly an amount to be sneered at all those years ago, but what was it compared to the dream of a lifetime? Unfortunately, my salary those days was also so pitiful that even this was too much for me. I requested my boss for a short-term loan and he gladly handed over the money which I passed on to Mejda and Munjal. The contribution of Sudha Murthy, of Rs. 10,000, during the formation of Infosys is the stuff corporate legends are made off; I do hope that S&T will also reach those heights and that in the footnotes of its organisational history, somewhere my little contribution will be acknowledged.

Over the years, there has probably, not been a single event worth mentioning in our family, happy or sad, that Munjal and Kaajal have not been an integral part of. Not as a guest, they have always been family taking on duties and responsibilities like few have. When Mamoni bid her final goodbye to us in November 2016, Munjal and Kaajal were on the next flight to Calcutta and stayed with us, for no less than ten days till all the rites and rituals had been gone through. Mamoni was every bit their mother, as she was ours; Kaku was in every way their father as he was ours.

In many a Hindi movie, I have heard the dialogue "Why could you not have been born out of my womb?" Munjal and Kaajal have proved, time and again, that to be a son or daughter, you do not have to be born out of somebody's womb.

My dearest friends – Abhik & Bubu

Ironic, is it not, that the two persons who have been my dearest friends, as a couple and as individuals over the last thirty-five years, are the only persons, apart from Munjal and Kaajal, amongst my close friends whose wedding I did not attend? C'est la vie.

I got to meet Abhik for the first time in Victoria House, when we used to enjoy our break during lunch hours. The thing about Abhik that blew me away was learning that he was a Higher Secondary ranking student (4th, if I am not mistaken). I have always had extreme admiration for people who excelled in academics; here was this guy who almost made it to the very pinnacle. Wow!

On top of this, he was well informed about most subjects, had balanced views on various topics but did not insist on thrusting his perspective down everyone's throat. To complete the picture, he was a music lover and cinema aficionado across multiple genres. In short, he was just the perfect guy. How could one not get drawn to a person like this?

By the time I got to know him well, he had got married to Anuradha (Bubu) a few days back. The memory of my first meeting with her still gets me chuckling; I have tried to recollect that episode elsewhere in this journal. Shortly after I got to know her, I learnt that she was a bright student of Economics, just a year junior to me in Jadavpur University, but what caught my fancy was something else. She was so piqued by missing out on the gold medal, by the narrowest of margins, that she decided to move from Economics to Accountancy, refusing to be tied down to her first love who had so unceremoniously ditched her. The loss of economists became the gain of the accountants. A fellow bull, a Taurean, in all its glory, she is.

Shortly thereafter, God gifted them with a darling daughter, Sonai (Subarna). This time, I did not miss out and I still remember going to visit Bubu and her little princess at Newlands Nursing Home. I use the term 'little' with deliberation; Sonai, being born a month ahead of time, was indeed a tiny infant and her size (or lack of it) took me by surprise. Coincidentally, our daughter, Chiki, was also born a month ahead of the scheduled date, but by this time, I was better prepared.

With each passing day, the bonds between the three of them and our family grew stronger, and it extended to include everybody around us. In times of happiness or grief, in times of celebration or despair, they have always been the first persons that I have reached out to. That dark morning in October 1994, when I saw my little brother lying lifeless at JCMC, the immediate response was to go to Abhik's place to catch my breath. Just taking one look at me, he realized that something was wrong. He calmed me down, understood what had happened and in his usual composed and practical manner, gave me a glass of milk and a few sweets as I would have a long day ahead. Words of sympathy and consolation would follow in due course, but he knew what had to be done, right then and there.

In life, you develop many friendly relationships. Some of them graduate to being friends, but **you need to be exceptionally fortunate to have friends like Abhik and Bubu**.

A touch of class – Sutapa Roy (Pinky)

When we lose somebody near and dear to us, and try to compose a eulogy in their honour, in their loving memory, we often tend to go overboard and deify the person who is no longer in our midst. When our dear Pinky, or Sutapa Roy, left us for the everlasting love of the Almighty, I put down my thoughts, carefully avoiding the temptation to portray her in any way other than exactly as I remember her.

"I still recall, vividly, that from the first day I saw you, that you came across as a lady different from all around you, used to walking with kings but never losing the common touch. In fact, it is incredibly difficult to separate Rudyard Kipling's immortal poem 'If', from the persona you were. Every couplet seemed to have been written with you in mind. How did you manage to never lose your cool, and maintain your *sang froid* regardless? I wish that I were privy to this secret.

It has been my proud privilege to call you my friend for 35 wonderful years. So much have I learnt from you – the true meaning of words we hear but seldom understand – elegance, class, integrity and purity are but only a small selection of a list that could go on and on. You had this unique ability to make everyone around you feel very special, even in a crowd. I am sure that today, everybody who had the pleasure of knowing you, from the liftman at Computer House to elite members of the corporate glitterati, however briefly, feels poorer for your departure from their lives.

One of the most enduring images in my mind is the sheer bliss visible on your face last year as I walked up to the 1st floor at FD-386. There I was, expecting to see you bravely fighting extreme physical discomfort and mental agony, considering all that you were going through. But lo and behold! The sight that greeted my eyes was the most loving grandmother you could ever hope to see, twirling around without a care in the world, holding aloft her darling Hiya, in a state of absolute ecstasy. They say life is but a collection of moments; I have rarely seen moments as precious as this.

While my heart goes out to DR, Coco, Mugdha, Mashima, Mrs. Paul, Bhaitu and Inti, amongst many others for this terrible loss, in many ways, the biggest loser has probably been little Hiya. It is so sad that she could not savour more time with her super special grandmother, but I am 100% sure that from wherever you are, you will always be little Hiya's guardian angel, holding her little hands and guiding her along the road called life.

The last 3 years have not been easy for you. You are now in peace. In God's loving arms, in everlasting love. It is a far, far better rest than you go to than you have ever known.

Fare thee well, our most dear and loved friend. **In our hearts, you will always remain.**"

The mystery lady

In life, most people and events can be understood, even if not completely agreed with. With careful scrutiny and hindsight, you can normally make sense of the train of events, and often empathise with the characters involved, even if it was not particularly pleasant when it did happen. In this section, I will try to describe, with as much honesty as I can gather, a life changing event that till date, I have not been able to fathom.

If somebody can help solve this for me, I shall remain eternally grateful.

Sometime towards the late eighties, I began to badger Mamoni about finding a life partner for me. Initially, she would just brush it off, saying that it would be like walking down the Hall of Shame, especially as most of my uncles and aunts had gone down the romantic route. An arranged marriage? Never. However, due to my insistence and demonstrated incapability of being able to find somebody who would say and hear the three magic words, she agreed to keep her eyes and ears open.

Around the summer of 1990, she bumped into an old acquaintance from her Digboi days at Calcutta Club. Exchanging memories, the question of how their children were doing, future plans etc. came up for discussion. Soon, it was evident that there was this bright boy who was looking for a life partner, and there was this sweet and pretty young girl wanting to 'settle down'. Why don't we see if things can work out? Why don't the boy and girl meet each other to see how they feel? Good idea.

Back from the Club, Mamoni called me for a chat on the subject and advised me to meet the girl. I was quite excited at the prospect, especially as there was the added romance of me flying down to Bombay and then catching an afternoon train to Pune to join the girl's family for dinner; quite a filmy touch, if you like. And within a few days, there I was at Pune station, being warmly received by my prospective in-laws, ahead of the dinner meeting with my prospective wife.

She came across much like the person I had imagined my wife to be; sharp features, beautiful eyes, pretty, academically accomplished and a professional to boot. On top of this, she was a good conversationalist, who injected just the right amount of self-deprecatory tones to show that she was not one to take herself too seriously. Things looked good, and my mind started racing forward to what could be.

Shortly after dinner was over, her mother called me aside and asked me how I felt about taking things forward. Naturally, I expressed my willingness, if not eagerness, to do so. At this point, her mother told me that there was something that she wanted to share with me, something that she had already discussed with Mamoni.

A few months prior to their meeting in the Club, the lady had just got out of a short-lived marriage with an IT professional, as there were issues about his past relationships continuing and other unsavoury stuff. I was also told that their marriage had not been consummated (as if these trivial things mattered in today's day and age) as things had blown up shortly after the marriage was solemnized. To support this claim, I was also shown a court decree that stated that their marriage had been terminated through annulment, not divorce. At this point, I did not even know what on earth annulment was, and how it was different from divorce.

Anyway, to cut a long story short, I was asked if this would affect my decision to proceed in the matter. Here, let me confess a weakness that exists in me, a weakness that I am quite proud of, strange as it may sound. Having come from a broken home, having seen women at the receiving end of innumerable social inequities, I have always harboured (and still do) an irrepressible desire, or urge, to be that somebody special for the lady in my life. Everybody gets married; how could I stand out from the crowd? Suddenly, in the post-dinner conversation with the lady and her mother, I had found what I was looking for. This was it, I thought.

Returning to Calcutta, I had a heart-to-heart chat with Mamoni. We agreed that this was something that needed to stay between the two of us, considering what the lady had already been through. As Kaku was a man with a conservative mindset, his own unconventional marriage notwithstanding, this was the best way to protect her and our marriage from any clouds of an irrelevant past casting shadows on our lives.

Onward to 12th May, 1991. On the auspicious day of Akshay Tritiya, we exchanged vows and tied the knot. When one of my dear friends, I think it was Debashis Roy, asked her how she felt shortly thereafter, the lady, in her inimitable laconic style responded "Warm" (a pun on the temperature and her mind) and we burst into laughter, appreciating her ready wit. Things looked good.

A couple of days later, as we were getting ready for the reception, I asked her for her jewelry, so that I could keep it in the almirah for safe keeping. Rather strangely, I thought, she asked me if I would be keeping the keys. When I said yes, she looked at me quizzically and asked why her ornaments should be kept in my custody. This shook me to the core, with its implied lack of trust. Nevertheless, I asked her to keep the keys if it made her feel any better, but truth be told, I was feeling shaken.

After the reception, we proceeded to Mahabaleswar for our honeymoon, accompanied by my in-laws. Strange, and unheard of, right? I thought so, too. For the purpose of brevity, and respecting our personal space, I will not go into the details. Suffice to say, she insisted on maintaining a more than normal distance from me, especially when we were by ourselves, which I found to be quite disturbing.

Back in Calcutta, she refused to sign, as the employee's wife, on the medical declaration form of my company on the plea that as she was not an employee of CESC, there was no justification for her to be covered by CESC's medical insurance schemes. Another day, as we were chatting on the verandah, I was, romantically caressing her hand. Suddenly, she withdrew it and said "I hope that you have had enough of playing with me". Somehow, red flags were popping all over the place.

One evening, Kaku came back from office, looking as black as death. I have heard this phrase before, but never thought that I would ever get to see this in real life. When he called me aside and asked me to sit down, I knew that something serious was coming up. Point blank, he told me that we had been cheated and that the lady had been married before. Her previous husband had come over to Kaku's office and shown him a bunch of their wedding photographs.

Clearing my throat, realizing that my worst fears had come true and that our (Mamoni's and mine) efforts to keep this issue under wraps had failed, I confessed that I was aware of her previous marriage. As was Mamoni. And that it was our joint decision to keep this away from everybody else. Kaku looked stunned. Stunned at me being aware of this but going ahead with the marriage (as I am also a person with a very strong rooting in traditional values), shocked beyond belief that his wife could be aware of this and not have shared it with him.

The lady got drawn into the conversation sometime during the evening and realized that things had become difficult. Very difficult. In sheer nervousness, she called her parents and asked them to come over to our home for dinner, the next day.

Here we were now at the dining table – Mamoni, Kaku, Chotloo, the lady, her mother and her father, with the food on the table being the last thing on anybody's mind. I do not remember much of the discussion itself; all I remember was that Kaku was withdrawn from the group, not participating in the conversation and being rather curt while responding to members of the lady's family. This was totally in contrast to the charming conversationalist that I have always known him to be.

After dinner, her parents suggested that given the present situation, it would be a good idea if she returned to Pune with her parents for a few days. They also asked if I would like to accompany her, to give her strength and be with her in her time of need. That familiar 'knight in shining armour' persona again popped up in my head, ignoring all her behavioural anomalies over the past few weeks. In my mind, the issue was crystal clear. Here was my wife, cornered and nervous, and I had to do whatever was required to protect her and stand by her side.

The next morning, I quietly packed her jewelry, collected my educational certificates and went to my office to write a three-line resignation letter. In effect, I was bidding farewell to my life in Calcutta, to my parents, brothers, friends and relatives, to be able to stand by my prime responsibility, my wife. It was a momentous decision, no doubt, but it was one that I had to take.

By the evening of that day, we were all on the lawns of my in-law's house, in distant Pune. Shortly thereafter, we started to think of our future options. They ranged from a job in Pune or Bombay, to migrating to USA where her brother was pursuing his higher studies. One evening, gazing out to the nearby hills, I mentioned to her that regardless of what the future held for us, the really important thing was that we were about to build a life together, aligned with each other's dreams.

To this, I got a reply that turned my blood to water, my knees to jelly. She said "Chotloo, come on. Just forget this sentimental wishy-washy talk. If we are thinking of going to USA now, it is because it suits you, suits me. That's it. The rest is all crap." In that one instant, the past couple of months just flashed by, in front of my eyes.

Here I was, having left my family, my job, my friends and relatives; essentially to be by my wife's side. And here was this lady, who far from acknowledging it and committing to a life together, had just casually brushed it off as a fly from her shoulder. At that moment, I realized that my life with her was over, before it had even started. All that I could hope to do was to get back to Calcutta, praying that life would give me a second chance.

This was in the middle of 1991. Things went rapidly downhill from here on and finally, after a year and half of painful logistics and tortuous legal proceedings, our break was formalized by the end of 1992.

A whole set of questions remain unanswered; they keep bothering me even after three decades.

The evergreen friends – Joyjit and Rupa Ghosh

If you are lucky, you find friends like Joyjit and Rupa. Only if you are very lucky.

When the TCS Utility group began expanding its presence in the sleepy town of Warrington towards the middle of 2002, amongst those who came over from Calcutta was this Ghosh family. No, I am not talking about our family; I refer to Joyjit, Rupa, Simba and Puma. What a family it was, is, and always will be.

The first time we went to their place, I saw Joyjit relaxing (or trying to, at least) on the sofa and there was this little creature, who was climbing up the rear surface. Without too much success, as he promptly collapsed back on to the carpet – thank God for its cushioning properties. Before too long, this same toddler was sliding down the banister, facing backwards. Who was this bundle of energy, this adorable ball? It was Puma, the younger scion of the Joyjit family.

While all this was going on, Rupa was scampering around the house, reprimanding her kids as if it made any difference. There was Joyjit phlegmatically taking the whole scene in. When I asked him if he realised that Puma could get hurt by his ongoing series of antics, he calmly informed me that just a couple of weeks back, he had fractured his arm. I had nothing further to say.

As we got to know them better, we realized that behind this lady who was frantically trying to maintain a semblance of order in her household, and the husband who had the detached air of someone who has seen it all before; lay a pair who did not understand the phrase "Sorry, we cannot do this." **Anything and everything, however unreasonable and demanding that it was, all you had to do was ask.**

I remember the time when we organized Chiki's birthday party in December 2002, where the list of invitees kept growing by the hour and stopped only when it had reached the humongous number of eighty. It was Rupa and Joyjit who, without even being requested to, promptly volunteered to take care of a couple of items to be cooked; which the two of them did, over the night, non-stop. This is what friends are made of, especially if they happen to be Joyjit and Rupa.

More recently, after we had moved to Saudi Arabia, Aditi's mother, uncle and aunt all contracted the dreaded Covid-19 virus simultaneously. At this time, this was a rampaging pandemic with support services having come to a virtual standstill. In this time of desperate need, the only person that I could reach out to was Joyjit.

Hearing of their predicament, he assured me that a solution would be found. Within hours, he called me, gave me a number of a reliable healthcare service provider experienced in treating Covid-19 patients, and that too, elderly patients as their care needs are different. Today, all three of them are doing fine, which definitely would not have been so, without his prompt and effective support.

Joyjit and Rupa, you have been the brick in the wall for us, for everybody around you.

Unforgettable Episodes

A selection of episodes that have refused to fade with the flux of time.

Dad – Carrying coals on his back (Dec 1954)

I am now going to discuss a part of Baba's life that I am kind of hazy about. It is quite possible that I may have got some of the facts wrong, and I request my readers to grant me this extra degree of latitude.

Shortly after Mejda was born in the winter of 1954, my parents were struggling to make both ends meet in the cold climes of London. Those days, hot water would be available by using piped gas as the source of energy, gas that was not free; it cost money. Every penny saved was a penny that could be used to buy bread, chicken or vegetables for the two babies.

Close to where he worked, there was an open coal yard, with nobody really bothering if someone took a bag or two from there. As you know, coal is rather heavy and coal dust has an awful tendency of coming out of jute bags to pollute the atmosphere. Consequently, you were not allowed to carry bags of coal in public transport systems, be it buses or the London Underground, the Tube.

On the other hand, hot water was a daily and critical need if the children were to survive the biting London winter. Having no other options, and being a strong man with a high sense of responsibility, Baba would fill up these jute bags with coal, and carry it on his back, all the way home, for his children to get the required hot water. Day after day, I am not sure for how long, this was the routine.

It is not difficult to understand where the extreme determination and mental strength that my brothers have shown throughout their lives, has come from.

It's all in the genes, dear friend.

Igloo – The missing Casanova (Feb 1967)

It was one more of the party nights at Digboi Club that my parents went out to attend. I am not sure about the year; it was probably 1966 or thereabouts. As was the normal practice, they left around eight p.m. By nine, all the children had turned in for the night. Or so it was thought.

It was a beautiful full moon night. On a cloudless sky, the glow of the moon was visible in all its glory on the plants and trees around our house, especially the majestic grapefruit trees and its muscular branches.

Maybe my parents came back a little earlier than expected that night, maybe not. Whatever be the case, Mamoni looked into the children's bedroom and one of the beds seemed to be filled in a little less than usual, the bed used by my eldest brother, Borda. Wondering what the matter could be, she walked up to the bed and was stunned to notice that in place of Borda, there were two carefully arranged pillows, in James Bond style, designed to look like a sleeping teenager. Immediately, she drew Baba's attention and together, they started looking all over the place for him.

Not finding him in the house, they came out to the garden, scratching their heads in sheer bewilderment. Suddenly, the luminous glow of the moon revealed a young couple, romantically engaged, high on one of the branches of the grapefruit tree. Before any other feelings came to the surface, I suspect that the first thought was one of incredulous surprise, of amazement at the sheer audacity of Borda and our neighbour's daughter, Chhanda.

What followed thereafter, would normally be enough to dampen the ardour of most wannabe Romeos, but our family Lothario was a different breed altogether. Physical lashings, often with the aid of leaf-stripped branches from the trees, could never deter him from his pranks, romantic or otherwise. **It was perhaps this extreme machismo that drew young ladies to him like flies to a flame.** For one thing was certain, this Romeo never wanted for a steady supply of dreamy-eyed Juliets.

Mejda and I have often discussed amongst ourselves how we could follow in his illustrious footsteps, but truth be told, we never even came close. It was only Baby who proved to be his worthy successor, but that is another story altogether.

Family – The rampaging pachyderms (May 1967)

During our stay in Digboi, life was good, as I have mentioned in quite a few places. Amongst the things that we liked to do, was to go for drives in the nearby jungles, occasionally catching sight of majestic elephants lazily strolling around in their own kingdom, swaying their trunks from one branch to another. You see an elephant at peace with itself, and you see nature at peace with the world at large. Tuskers, matriarchs and calves walking down the jungle paths was a common sight that we were used to, and in fact, looked forward to seeing.

One winter evening, we were invited to a wedding feast, to a place that lay on the other side of the jungle. That did not bother us, as we would frequently go through it. Just to give you an idea, the jungles around Digboi had a few asphalt roads, surrounded by dense undergrowth on either side. The roads themselves were well laid, but did not have too much leeway in terms of width. Overtaking the car in front of you was, normally, not an option.

We started late in the afternoon, just as darkness was beginning to descend. By the time we hit the jungle, natural light had faded and the car headlights had to be switched on. About ten minutes into the jungle, as we were approaching a corner, we saw a herd of elephants, all matriarchs, huddled around a calf that was groaning in pain. Probably, it had been attacked by a passing leopard looking for an easy meal. We felt sad for the calf and just as sad for the mother and aunts. We put in a short prayer for the calf, for its recovery, and moved on.

Dinner was good; the company was even better. By the time we bid goodbye to our gracious hosts, it had become dark, with the woods being pitch dark thanks to the dense foliage around us. On the way back, when we came to the same spot where we had earlier seen the calf groaning, we noted that it now lay on its side, tragically lifeless. The herd around it had grown in numbers and now included a huge tusker, as impressive as it was frightening. All of them looked disturbed, shaking their heads vigorously from side to side. By the way, elephants are amongst the most emotional of wild animals; they are the only species to kiss tenderly with their trunks, apart from human beings.

When they are angry, things are oh, so totally different. If you have ever had the misfortune of coming across an elephant in 'mast' (in season), you are lucky to have survived to read this. Not to the same degree, but a herd of elephants in anger, or extreme grief, is also not something you want to come across. Realizing that we were in dangerous territory, Baba tried to cross this herd as quietly as possible, trying his best not to draw their attention to our car. His best was not good enough.

Without any warning whatsoever, just after we passed the herd, the male tusker raised his trunk skywards and let out a thunderous bellow. That was enough for the full herd to be galvanized into immediate action, and our tiny car became the focal point of their pent-up anger and sorrow. We were suddenly transformed, in the eyes of the grief-stricken elephants, from an innocent group of travelers to this murderous bunch of villains, who had to be trampled into the dust. As Baba stepped on the accelerator, so did these huge monsters behind us.

Driving at high speed through these jungle roads was not a very safe option, due to the dense undergrowth on both sides that had virtually merged into the road in the darkness. I am not sure that road safety was anywhere near the top of Baba's agenda at this point of time. The ground beneath the car reverberating under the weight of these charging goliaths does have a way of changing your priorities, we realized.

Just as it seemed that we would be successful in outpacing them, another curve ball was thrown at us. Shortly after we took a sharp corner, to our mind-numbing horror, we saw a large timber-laden truck directly in front of us. Blissfully unaware of the drama that was being unfolded behind it, the truck was moving along at a leisurely pace, the kind of speed you would normally expect it to be cruising at, late at night, on jungle roads. Honking as loudly and frequently as he could, Baba realized that it was of no use whatsoever.

By this time, the body temperature of both Baby and me had shot up to 105° and Mamoni was frantically calling upon all the gods and goddesses there were in the Hindu pantheon. Borda and Mejda were frozen stiff with terror, as with every passing second, these giants seemed to be gaining on us, till we could almost see the wrinkles on their skin and the murderous rage in their eyes. Even now, as I punch out these words on my laptop, I can recall the terror we felt that day, a terror like we have probably never felt thereafter.

Ultimately, Baba had only one throw of the die left. It was now or never. Flooring the accelerator, he swerved to the right, praying that there would be asphalt surface just enough for us to stay on the road, and not the dense undergrowth. God was on our side, and somehow, he managed to overtake the lorry in front. I do not remember anything of what happened thereafter. How did Baba regain his composure, how did Mamoni thank the gods or for that matter, how did our body temperatures come back to normal, or how long it took, I have absolutely no idea.

Somewhere, in the eyes of those rampaging elephants, I think that I have seen the face of death. I would not like to see that again, till it is time for the final countdown.

Igloo & Bigloo – The Good, The Bad and The Ugly (Jul 1967)

Earlier in this collection of memories, I have referred to the crazy escapades of Borda and Mejda, especially during the nine years or so that we spent in the oil township of Digboi. Here, allow me to recount one of them in greater detail.

The Good, The Bad and The Ugly. This was a spaghetti Western released in the mid-sixties, which appealed to young teenagers tremendously, especially their thirst for daring deeds and adventures. Borda and Mejda were no exception to this, but then they decided to take it one step further. They were so enamoured by the Clint Eastwood & Eli Wallach acts of rescuing the about to be hanged convict by shooting the rope, that they decided to re-enact the hanging scene in our garden. There was a tall grapefruit tree along with its sturdy branches which provided just the ideal setting for what they had in mind.

They got a short stool and placed it under one of the more impressive looking branches, as it would have to support the weight of the victim. Borda convinced Mejda that the hanging would only be for a short period of time, and that he would be 'rescued' very quickly. On one of the few occasions that he suffered a total brain fade, Mejda agreed to play the victim's role. A noose was loosely tied around his neck, and all was set for the ultimate action sequence to get rolling.

On the other side of the garden, lived our neighbours. The lady of the house, having completed her morning chores, was enjoying a relaxing bath, soap bubbles, loofahs and all. Suddenly, out of the corner of her eye, she saw this absolutely unbelievable scene taking shape just twenty-five feet away. Without taking any time to think, or bothering to scream, caring not that she did not even have the proverbial fig leaf to cover her modesty, she just made a wild dash for the grapefruit tree. Just as Borda's well aimed kick was about to dislodge the stool under Mejda, she dived forward and embraced Mejda in her arms.

What happened thereafter, I will leave to the reader's imagination. All that I can say is that the rest of the day did not turn out to be pleasant for either of the brothers. If Mejda is today living his dream, **I hope that, at least once in a while, he does remember the lady who just may have made it possible.**

Chotloo – Did you have a full dinner? (Aug 1968)

As is common in small townships, life revolved around the workplace during the day and social gatherings after dusk. My parents too had a fairly active evening life that often stretched to the late hours of the night. At the same time, being rather strict sticklers for discipline, arrangements would always be made for the children to be fed and sent to bed at the regular time, regardless of their presence or absence.

Sometime in the middle of 1968, my parents were invited to a pretty big social event at the local Digboi Club, the hip hop happening place those days. My mother had given strict instructions to our nanny to ensure that all the brothers were properly fed and packed off to bed by nine p.m. As my aunt, Khukuma, was staying with us those days, she was requested to oversee this operation to its logical conclusion.

In this respect, please note that for me, being the boy with a healthy appetite and the most favoured child, dinner was a structured meal starting with a soup, and going down to dal, vegetables, main dish and a sweet dish. Why? For a balanced meal, of course, for all-round development of mind and body. No wonder, those days, I often looked like a baby elephant.

As the evening rolled on, dinner was served and we proceeded to polish off what was a tasty meal of rice and mutton curry, accompanied by dal and vegetables. Being the apple of my mother's eye, both the ladies made sure that my plate was heaped and refilled continuously. With the nanny manning the supply function and my aunt lovingly handing them down my hungry mouth, it was a meal to savour. Soon, as all good things must, this feast came to an end. My stomach and brain combined to scream 'Enough'. Both the ladies looked pleased with their efforts as I became impatient to go to bed and sleep the sleep of a fully contented boy.

But wait! Suddenly, my aunt's face took on a strange look. A look of 'Oh my God, what have we done?' was writ right across it. Perplexed, the nanny asked her what was amiss. My aunt reminded her that my mother had specifically asked them to make sure that I had my end-of-meal sweet dish, comprising a bowl of rice, milk and mashed bananas. But how on earth, could I be given even a single morsel of food, as I was already groaning as any hugely overfed boy would?

Seeing that I was sleepy as well, they somehow convinced me to gulp down a few morsels of this dessert, all the time being fearful of me throwing up or worse. After a while, making sure that all was well, both of them retired for the night, thanking their stars for a miraculous escape.

Late that night, my parents returned and as was customary, came into the children's bedroom to give us a goodnight hug and tuck us in. As I was still recovering from the excesses of dinner, I had not fully transitioned into slumber land, but lay wandering on the boundaries somewhere. When Mamoni saw me, sleepy but not fully asleep, she casually enquired, "Chotloo, did you have a full dinner?" From somewhere in my half-sleepy state, my mouth responded, "No, Mamoni. I am feeling hungry".

My aunt and nanny, who were hanging around in the vicinity, stood aghast, not believing what they had just heard. To say blood rushed to their faces would be an understatement. Responding to the unspoken question of my mother, both of them could only make some totally unintelligible noises before fleeing the scene.

For the next few days, suffice to say that I kept my distance from both of them. **Even today, memories of this unforgettable anecdote have us in splits.**

Baby – Throat constriction (Nov 1968)

Baby had everything going his way for the first few years of his life. Starting life's journey in the private cabin of Calcutta's most luxurious nursing home, having an ayah dedicated to look after him within days of his birth, flying down to oil-rich Digboi as soon as the doctors allowed him to, life was good.

The incident I will relate now occurred when he was about four years old, an adorable toddler who charmed everybody with his easy smile and pained looks, if anything did not meet his total approval. He was the darling of the house. To be honest, this was also leading to an annoying streak of being spoilt, what with everyone pampering him no end. One area which was getting to be slightly more so, was his increasingly finicky nature about food. Anything that did not delight his taste buds was just refused to be consumed. His nanny, Asha Mashi, often had a hard time making everything go down his throat, as she had clear instructions as to what, how much and when, had to be fed to Baby.

Around this time, my aunt, Khukuma came to stay with us along with her husband, Khokon Kaku and her two-year-old son, Mithu. She is a loving soul, as warm hearted as you could be, but not tolerant of antics, be they of adults or children. For a few days, she observed Baby's ability to wriggle out of eating anything that was not to his liking, with nobody being able to do anything about it. She sat down and thought hard, to find a way out of this impasse.

After a few days, when he was up to his usual tricks, Khukuma went up to him and asked him why he was not eating the food. Baby responded that it was not a question of not eating the food, but rather an issue of **not being able to eat** the food.

When Khukuma wondered what the reason could be, Baby, with all his childish innocence, replied that his throat had become too small for the food to go down. Hearing this perfectly logical answer, Khukuma was blown away, but only momentarily. She called Borda and Mejda, and asked them to get a hot iron rod.

Baby, who was feeling smugly confident till this point, was suddenly bemused. Hesitantly, he asked what the rods were there for. In a tone dripping with honey, she explained that his throat had become small; inserting the hot iron rod down the throat would enlarge it. Then he would have no difficulty in eating his food.

His angelic eyes now lit up wondering that she couldn't be serious, could she? To dispel all doubts, he saw my brothers carrying a long rod in their hands, approaching him in all seriousness. Suddenly, his mind cleared. Desperate situations call for desperate remedies. After coughing out loudly a couple of times, he told Khukuma "I think my throat has become bigger. Maybe, I can eat the food now." She agreed to try putting one morsel into his mouth, and guess what? It went like water down a chute. So did the next, and the one thereafter.

The problem of the constricted throat was solved, once and for all.

Parents – Break-up of their marriage (Feb 1969)

By the late sixties, the marriage between my father and mother had turned sour, for reasons that I would rather not get into here. Not to mince words, there was a wide gulf between the two in terms of personal charm, educational qualifications, work profile and physical attractiveness. If one was an honest to earth mid-level technical support executive, the other was a glamorous surgeon, the cynosure of society at large. If one was a person whose values were grounded in middle class and semi-feudalistic stereotypes, the other was one who was chafing to embrace modernity and all that it stood for.

To compound matters further, there was a significant gulf in earnings, something that is still difficult for an Indian male to accept, not to speak of what it must have been nearly six decades ago. I believe that all these factors led to a complex developing in my father's mind along with a heightened sense of insecurity, his external stoicism and bravado notwithstanding.

This resulted in an increasing frequency of heated arguments which, unfortunately and unacceptably, regardless of the triggers, degenerated into episodes of domestic violence. Agreed, these instances were always followed by extreme contrition and attempts to make up in as loving a manner as possible. However, the cumulative effect of hot and cold often leaves the skin burnt.

As my mother explained to me much later, there was a huge reservoir of love in my father. Nobody could be as romantic as him, but to live with him any longer had just ceased to be a viable option. In her own words, things had reached a point towards the late sixties that it was a question of when, and with whom, she would leave my father, not if. The most difficult and heart-wrenching part of this decision was that she knew it would mean leaving her children behind, the four jewels of her heart. The laws of society and marital courts were heavily skewed in favour of the father retaining full custody in cases of divorce, which was then a virtually unknown word, especially in society, if not in the court rooms.

At this juncture, came into our life, this suave, polished and charming gentleman called Bivash Chandra Maitra, as my father's boss. He was much younger than both my parents. The rest, as they say, is history.

If I have kept the narrative of this life changing event brief, it is for two reasons.

Firstly, I was too young at the time events unfolded to understand what on earth was going on. I have heard Mamoni's account in my later years, but never got a chance to understand Baba's point of view. As they say, in any disputed or inflammatory issue, there are three sides to the story; my version, your version and the real version.

Secondly, and more importantly, the development or decay of a marriage is as intensely a personal matter between the husband and wife as any relationship can ever get. I do not believe that anybody, not the children, parents or siblings, have any right to poke their nose into places they have no business to, beyond providing the necessary support to their loved ones, as may be required.

There was one tragic incident that I need to mention here. I call it tragic, as it was totally avoidable. If only people had managed to stay within their boundaries and not interfered in the lives of others, who knows how things would have panned out.

I have been given to understand that shortly before he left us forever, my parents were on the verge of giving their fractured marriage one last go, letting bygones be bygones. Granted, there were huge issues to be resolved before that could happen, issues of trust and security. The fact that this was even on the table, was something that was just awesome, especially for us brothers. Scars would be healed, if not erased, with the passage of time. Could anything be better?

Baba had grown to be heavily dependent on his close relatives for the support that they had given him during this difficult phase of his life, and for the affection they had showered on his 'mother-less' children. Also, his confidence was probably shaken to the extent that he needed to consult with them before moving forward.

Apparently, the advice he got was this; Mamoni had erred grievously in leaving Baba and should seek forgiveness before she could be accepted into the family once again. Given the gravity of her 'sins' and the public humiliation that the family had faced, the repentance also needed to be a public spectacle. *She would have to rub her nose, along the ground, all the way from the children's park to our house, in public.*

This was something that no self-respecting person would ever consider doing, and definitely not Mamoni, being the person she was. The condition was so ridiculous that even those laying it down knew that it would be rejected out of sight. In the process, it destroyed forever, any chance whatsoever of Baba getting back together with his beloved wife. This condition was laid down by the very people who worshipped the ground that she walked on, who had benefited from her largesse and support in so many ways over the years. Just unbelievable, it simply blows your mind. What was gained by this, I do not understand and frankly, at this point of my life, neither do I care. **What remains forever, is that I will never forget. Forgive, maybe but forget, never.**

There is one final point to ponder. How has the past affected my own life's journey, I wonder? Possibly, it has done so in two ways.

One, it has helped me develop a steely resolve that no matter what, my children will never, ever have to face the insecurity, if not terror, of living in a fractured home. I owe the Almighty a huge debt as He has ensured this; in Aditi, I have got a partner who has been with me, all the way, through all of life's twists and turns.

Two, the uncertainty on multiple fronts faced during my formative years has, in all likelihood, reduced my risk-taking capacity quite significantly. 'If it ain't broke, do not fix it' has become a guiding mantra for me. While this has ensured a relatively stable ride, I must confess that this attitude has possibly nudged me into accepting sub-optimal situations somewhat. If I were to look back and introspect, if I have been able to do full justice to the gifts that He has bestowed on me, the answer will probably have to be 'not as much as I could have, should have'.

However, when all is said and done, even if more is said than done, I am grateful to Him for all that He has given us, done for us and continues to do so.

Relatives – Just not done (Apr 1970)

Let me tell you about a mother who had four young boys. The two elder boys would continuously be hanging around their mother, telling her that just like crabs, they could move around only by clinging on to her back. The third boy was the darling of his parents as he was always obedient, had a healthy appetite, used to bring in good grades and could not dream of a world which did not have his mother as its epicenter. Finally, there was this six-year-old kid, who did not even understand that there was a world beyond his mother.

When, for reasons beyond them, they found themselves separated from their mother, their dear Mamoni, they were bewildered. What on earth was happening? How could she stay away from them, how could they live without her? Nature abhors a vacuum, and answers rushed in from people around them, all save Baba who was the only person who could have provided any cogent and honest answers.

It is not difficult to understand that this outpouring of negative thoughts and feelings was triggered by the fact that till recently, Mamoni was the apple of their eyes, a person who was revered like few have been. It was just incomprehensible to them how Mamoni could snap her ties with the family, little realizing that this was (a) not a spontaneous decision at all, and (b) it really had nothing to do with them. On closer reflection, it was a perfect demonstration of how close intense love and hatred are to each other; love spurned turns into hatred. A pity that this was not understood and appreciated, but then again, marriages breaking up was such a rarity those days, it is understandable, though not at all justifiable.

Before too long, these children were fed stories and God knows what awful stuff about how selfish, heartless and uncaring their mother was, their darling Mamoni was. Not knowing or understanding any better, these impressionable minds were gradually convinced that if life had suddenly turned on its head for them, it was their bad mother (note, no longer the term of endearment 'Mamoni' which literally meant the jewel amongst mothers) who lay at the root of it all.

This was the same person who would splurge her full pay cheque to buy a return ticket from Bombay (where she was now working with the Ministry of Health) to come to Calcutta to visit her children, but would often be rudely sent away by the domestic help. This was the same person who would go to the nearby children's park where her children played in the evenings, in the hope of spending a precious hour, holding them close, if allowed to. This was the same person whose heart would be shred into pieces when she heard her son confess that he could not have hot lunches at school as they were too expensive. I could go on and on ...

What did she get in return? Forget the insults and rebuffs from the very people who loved and admired her till recently; even her own child, that's me, (I hang my head down in shame to admit it), prayed that one of the flights that she travelled on, would crash, that she would go down in flames and be erased from our lives forever.

God, how can you ever forgive me for harbouring these vile thoughts against my creator and my life sustainer? I have confessed this to Mamoni. As only mothers can, she understood my pain and forgave me, soothing my troubled soul, caressing my hair with her hands and holding me close to her bosom.

In life, there are many wrongs and crimes. I wonder if any of them can surpass that of planting or nurturing negative thoughts in the mind of a child against his parent. Whether this be in the form of omission or commission, it makes little difference.

It is just not done.

Chotloo – Reading books in a book store (May 1970)

During the days in New Alipur, when life often seemed to be too depressing and painful to bear, I had two major escape routes. One, as discussed elsewhere, was going off to Bunu Pipi's house to unburden myself and chat with her covering all possible subjects and events. The other, strange as it may sound, was the neighbourhood book store, New Alipur Book House.

Shortly after getting admitted to Calcutta Boys School, along with Baba, I went there to get my new books, note books and stationery. Those days, this book store was a small shop, with an attractive display window, a medium-sized sales counter, a few cupboards on the ground floor and a spacious loft on the first floor. Connecting the sales counter to the loft, there was a wooden staircase.

The store was owned and manned by two brothers, both of whom looked strikingly similar and had identical charming smiles. The only difference between them was that the elder brother was significantly taller than his younger sibling. I am not sure whether it was during this first visit or a subsequent one, I was struck by the speed at which the younger brother would scoot up and down the stairs to the loft to get any book required by customers. My inquisitive eyes also realized that up in the loft, lay a treasure trove of books, freshly printed, covering subjects ranging from nature to wildlife, from tales of kings and warriors to mountains and seas.

Catching a glimpse of my wistfully wandering eyes, the elder brother asked me if I would like to go up to the loft and take a look. Before he had a chance to even reconsider his offer, and even as my father was making polite noises about what's the need and stuff, I had already scampered up the stairs and settled down, soaking in the sights and smells of this heaven in front of me.

For the next three years, as long as we were in New Alipur, **this became my favourite hideaway** and the two brothers developed a fondness for me that was matched, in full measure, by my gratitude towards them.

Tani & co – A picnic on the asbestos roof (Jun 1970)

It was a bright summer morning and the gang decided on a picnic. There was nothing remarkable about this, except that this picnic would be on top of an asbestos sheet which covered a small opening on the 2nd floor roof of our New Alipur house.

Around eleven in the morning, the gang (Tani, Apu, Panku, Dolly, Archana and I) got our sandwiches, cold drinks and chips and carefully climbed a rickety ladder, before slowly crawling our way to the end of the roof that was directly above a staircase landing. I am not sure of the sequence we did it in, but when the last of us had just about reached our dining spot, the asbestos sheet, or roof if you can call it that, decided that enough was enough and just collapsed.

A moment earlier, you had a bunch of neatly dressed girls and a boy all set to tuck into their midday goodies. The very next, they were crashing down to the staircase landing below.

Fortunately for us, and unfortunately for Panku, who was the 'healthiest' if you know what I mean, she was the first to hit the floor on her well-cushioned bottom. The rest of us had a much safer lap landing, on her.

Within a short while, we realized that apart from seriously bruised egos, a few minor cuts and bruises, dust and one pair of slightly hurt fundaments (Panku's), there was not too much damage. Nobody was seriously hurt, and that was a minor miracle. Regarding the asbestos roof itself, the less said the better. It lay in splinters of varying shapes and sizes, and we were very lucky that nobody was hit by them; somebody could have been badly injured. After dusting ourselves, with the visions of a summer picnic lying in ruins, we made our way to our respective homes.

Tani and I, we just had to get down from the landing to the first floor, while Apu had to go down to the ground floor, being our tenant. Amidst all the commotion, the seniors of the house came running, to see what was happening, and for a while, could not believe their eyes. Baba was amongst the first to recover, if an explosion of anger could be called recovery.

He took me to our bedroom, and **for the first and only time in my life, I was at the receiving end of a beating from him**. He got hold of a bamboo stick and hit me, hard, across my thighs. It left a scar that remains till this day. Tani too, got her fair share of hits; Baba could not be faulted for being partial. Looking back, I realize that it was not just anger at our recklessness, but naked fear at what could have happened, that triggered a reaction as violent as it was. Along with anger, there was a lot of love.

There was an amusing epilogue to this incident. Those days, Kaku, Tani's father, used to work long hours in one of the well-known hotels of Calcutta. Consequently, he used to come back home from work late, have dinner and then retire for the night. To avoid him getting agitated about the asbestos roof and the miraculous escape of us brats, he was not informed of the incident for quite a few days.

On a full moon night, while having dinner, he suddenly realized that the dining table and its contents were being lit by a glow that was far too beautiful to be coming from the incandescent lights inside the room. Casually, he looked around and noticed the beautiful moon bathing the dining room with its luminescence. He turned around and asked Thamma, who was serving him dinner, "Ma, how is it that we are enjoying this amazing beauty of moonlight from within the confines of the dining room?"

Fortunately, quite a few days had elapsed after the incident, and the matter was laughed off. If it had happened closer to the day, I suspect that both Tani and I would have had to endure a second round of corporal punishment.

Chotloo – Walking it from school (Feb 1971)

The day began like any other, during our stay in New Alipur. Mejda and I left for school. Around lunch time, we heard a lot of commotion in the neighbourhood, overflowing from the Moulali area across the red boundary walls of our school.

Somewhere in the central business district of Calcutta, an elderly politician, Hemanta Kumar Basu, was cruelly hacked down in broad daylight by his political adversaries. This, while being a heinous act by itself, was now a perfectly good reason for political activists, or gundaas, if you like, to bring the entire city to a standstill with no consideration whatsoever for the millions who had absolutely nothing to do with it. Within a few minutes, our school decided to close for the day and asked all students to vacate the premises immediately.

It was all fine, if the situation could in any way be called fine, but we had a minor technical problem. All public transport was off the roads and local trains had stopped running. I do not remember why, but Baba could not pick us up from school and bring us home. So, what could we do?

There were a few taxis plying but, Mejda had only Re 0.50 in his pocket (to cover the return bus fare for the two of us) and nothing more. The only other option, unpalatable if not unthinkable, was to walk all the way home, and that too by taking a circuitous route to avoid known trouble spots along the way.

Initially, our mood was one of irritation at what we thought to be an unnecessary bother for the day. Although we were used to the bus journey from school to our home taking the better part of an hour, we did not fully realise the time differential between a bus journey and a trudging walk with fully loaded school bags. Thank God, it was a relatively cool day in February. I use the term relatively only after looking at the calendar, for my memories of that day cannot find anything cool or pleasant.

From the school to the Ganges riverfront, and then crossing countless junctions, avoiding crowds, the walk continued on and on. Every once in a while, I would look hopefully towards Mejda and he would assure me that we had already covered most of the distance; that our home was just a short distance away. After a few rounds, I became wiser, if increasingly more despondent. We may have stopped on the way to wet our parched throats with a glass of lemon juice bought with the bus fare saved, but I am not sure.

At the end of what seemed to be forever, we reached home. And just collapsed. We had absolutely no energy to talk, eat or recollect what we had just been through. Somehow, we went for a bath and after that, I can remember nothing. I have been told that I was delirious for about three days thereafter, and it was only a series of cold compresses and refreshing baths that brought me back to reality. To think that two years to the day, before this pleasant mid-day walk covering about twelve kilometres in the sun, we were living the life of kings, in the lap of luxury.

Time does teach you a few lessons, when you least expect it. This, my friends, is the eternal circle of life.

Baba – Alladin's cave (May 1971)

During our days in New Alipur, during the difficult days when money was more a concept than a reality for us, let me recount an episode that provided one of the brighter sparks. To add to the spice quotient, let me try to tell it from the point of view of my partner in the episode, Tani.

"Near the children's park where we would go to play in the evenings, there was a hole-in-the-wall shop that used to sell chocolates, jelly beans, chewing gum and stuff that appealed to young boys and girls, people like Chotloo and me. The item that attracted us the most was this chocolate ball, wrapped in brightly-coloured glossy paper, that was too delicious for words. The only problem was that it cost a princely sum of Re 0.10 per piece, and we never had anything like money in our pockets.

One day, while we were crossing this shop on the way back home, and I was wistfully gazing at these goodies from the corner of my eye, Chotloo asked me if I would like to have one. Of course, I jumped at the offer and started slurping on it in no time, almost before he could pay the shop keeper. Before too long, the chocolate had disappeared, but my heart wanted more.

What was to be done? As I began to turn, taking a long last look at the glass container full of them, Chotloo asked "Would you like to have another one?" This time, I just could not believe my ears. While the second piece was also devoured as quickly as could be, what was the secret behind the infinite well of money that he must have come across?

He simply refused to reveal the whereabouts of his private Alladin's cave. After a lot of cajoling, coaxing and employing all tricks imaginable, he agreed to share his secret, but on a virtual oath of silence.

Jethu (Chotloo's father) had this habit of accumulating coins in his trouser pocket, which he would empty under the mattress before going to sleep. The next day, while getting ready for work, he would scoop the coins into his trouser pockets. This was noted by Chotloo in his usual unobtrusive but sly manner.

When Jethu got up from sleep for his morning shave and other morning activities, he would gently raise the mattress and take out a couple of coins from the bunch, being careful to select only the high value coins. This ensured value, without impacting the volume that Jethu would feel when he scooped the bunch back into his pocket. And therein lay the secret of his Alladin's cave.

The ironic part is that everybody had branded Borda, Mejda and me as the rascals of the family, with Chotloo being the goody-goody boy who could do no wrong."

Just goes to show, I guess, how important creating a proper brand image can be, throughout your life, in every sphere.

Mamoni and Baba – Never-ending love (Feb 1972)

This journal will never be anything like complete, if it did not reflect the love my parents had for each other, in their own ways. Even if they decided that they could not spend more than seventeen years together, some in ecstasy, some in agony and a few somewhere in between, their mutual love remained as strong as ever.

When Baba realized that his days were almost done, who did he turn to, to take care of his children? Not his brothers or sisters; he had full faith only in his beloved wife. A few days before he left us, when Mamoni came to visit him, Baba asked her categorically to take care of the four of us, as only in her did he see the strength and love required to be able to do this.

After his death, I have frequently had long conversations with Mamoni about him and the kind of person he was. Always, her refrain was the same. There was nobody on earth who could love her the way he could and did; there was nobody who could sacrifice as much for her as he could. If it had not been for his tragic trait of uncontrolled violence, there was not a man who could even hold a light to him. These words are not mine; they are all Mamoni's. I have just tried to put them down on paper, as best as I could.

Coming now to Baba, it was suggested, or so I have been given to understand, that he might think of re-marriage. His response was typical of a man who may have been separated from his wife, but who still loved her no end. Without a moment's thought, he asked whoever had come up with the idea never to bring this subject up again; he could not imagine being with anybody other than his dear Jharna.

Amongst my most vivid memories of Baba during the last years of his life, was of him sitting in the verandah, looking vacantly out into the dark skies, thinking of what could have

114

been or of what he had, with the one and only love of his life, Jharna. Puffing on his Panama cigarettes endlessly, often lighting one with the burning embers of the previous one, it was as if he could not bear to live without her any more. I remember that he had a service revolver with him. If he did not blow his brains out with it, it was simply because of his love for us, his concern for our future.

The agony that he went through, day after day, I have seen from close quarters, sitting quietly and helplessly by his side. There would I be, inhaling the rich flavour of unfiltered tobacco mingled with the unbearable pain of a man desperately in love with his wife who had left him.

If in later years I have been able to understand either Othello or Guru Dutt, and their personal anguish, a little more than others, this was where it began. What love and devotion are, what they mean beyond being a couple of four-letter and eight-letter words, I have learnt from my parents. Richard Burton and Elizabeth Taylor could not stay married to each other, but their love is the kind that the ages will remember.

On a smaller stage, my parents will always occupy a similar position in my eyes. **Somewhere in the heavens, I like to believe that they just may be rekindling their flames, as we speak.**

Baba – The last supper (Mar 1972)

Baba's days with us were numbered; only thing is that we did not know it.

Early in March 1972, we went to Thamma's brother's place for a family get-together over lunch. After enjoying a typically delicious meal, we were relaxing in the drawing room, chatting about this and that. Suddenly, Thamma's brother, who also happened to be a doctor, noticed something strange on Baba's forearm. There were red splotchy marks on his hand, which looked out of place and abnormal to a medical practitioner's eye. Checking his blood pressure, he saw that it was 220/110 mm of mercury, far too high to be acceptable. He asked Baba about other symptoms and at the end of it all, it was decided that there could be no further delay; supervised medical treatment had to start the very next day. A few tests were conducted and medication was started right away.

After a few days, Mamoni came to Calcutta and met Baba. During the course of their discussions, he mentioned what had transpired recently. Mamoni, on hearing what she did, checked out a few things herself and realized that things had reached a critical stage. She advised him to get hospitalized immediately.

Although she did not tell him this, while talking about that evening with me a long time afterwards, she recalled that one of the symptoms Baba specifically mentioned was the pain he kept feeling towards his lower back. Mamoni recognised this as a symptom of acute kidney failure, possibly caused by his history of malignant hypertension. As she put it to me, "At that moment, I knew that we were talking weeks, not months'". She has always had an amazing medical acumen. This time too, unfortunately for us, she was deadly accurate in her prognosis.

By this time, Baba had got his inner senses working overtime; he probably had the feeling that he did not have too much time left. Suddenly, he invited all members of his extended family, about twenty-five of them, for lunch on Sunday, 5th March. As I have highlighted elsewhere, we lived in an environment of extreme financial stringency, from the first day of the month to the last. This was, at that point of time, an inexplicable extravagance, particularly as there was no specific occasion to be celebrated, and came as a huge surprise to all of us.

If I remember correctly, the menu was quite lavish (pulao, mutton (lots of it), fried brinjal, vegetables, chutney, sweets); it was as if it was a wedding feast. In my entire stay during the 69 to 72 period, the only meal that could compare with this one, was the feast we had at the time of Pipi's wedding.

Little did we realize then, that this was his way of bidding us goodbye. Deep in his heart, he probably felt that his time on Planet Earth was now at an end. **Seventy-two hours after lunch that Sunday, Baba left us forever, for his heavenly abode.**

Kaku – The mother of all welcomes (Mar 1972)

On 24th March, 1972, began a whole new life for Baby and me.

Leaving the traumatic days of our stay in New Alipur behind, and having lost our father just sixteen days back, here we were on the verge of a whole new world. The previous day, Mamoni had taken us to New Market to buy clothes, footwear and goodies for us, in the true style of the Digboi days, to help us shed the pained and despondent persona that the last three years had forced down on us.

We were also excited at the prospect of travelling by air, and that too not once but three times within a day, from Calcutta to Vizag to Vijaywada and finally, to Hyderabad. In those days, hopping flights were just opportunities to enjoy the thrill of taking off and landing; the more, the merrier.

On the last leg of our journey, shortly before we commenced our descent to the city of pearls, Charminar and kebabs, the pilot invited Baby and me to come to the cockpit to view the landing. Oh! What a sight it was! As the altimeter moved towards zero, the splendor of the city below, swathed in blue and yellow lights, lay with its arms spread wide and inviting, waiting to welcome its newest inhabitants. That was a sight that will always be embedded in my heart. More was to come. Much more.

As we disembarked from the aircraft and made our way to the arrival lounge, we saw this handsome, elegantly dressed gentleman waving to us, beaming from ear to ear, holding one of the biggest bouquets that you will ever see.

We knew him briefly from our days in Digboi. Over the duration of our stay in Calcutta, he had been transformed into an absolute monster in our eyes. But what and who were we seeing now? This gentleman bore little resemblance to the image we had in our minds. Surprises will never cease.

Our house in Somajiguda was atop a hillock, not too far from the airport. After a short ride, we drove in to the patio of our house and walked in to a spacious and well decorated drawing-cum-dining room. What took our breath away, in more ways than you can possibly imagine, were the amazing sights and smells.

Right across the hallway, there was this huge sign decorated by colourful balloons that shouted "Welcome home, Chotloo and Babyloo". On the dining table, lay a sumptuous feast; chicken biryani, mutton kababs, kalakand etc. Crockery and cutlery neatly laid out along with freshly starched napkins, place mats, crystal glasses; it was a table fit for royalty.

And for whom? Two boys who just a few days back, did not have the foggiest idea of what the future held for them, whose relatives had raised the question of who would meet their expenses, who for the last two weeks had been roaming around the city in unstitched garments and rubber sandals, eating only semi-cooked food?

Was this for real, or was this just another celestial prank being played? To say that **we were dumbfounded, just blown away by what lay before our eyes and senses**, would be putting it in the mildest possible way. If this was not enough, we were taken to our bedroom to freshen up, and change for dinner. But wait, where was the bedroom? We could not see it at all, as the bed, the floor, the cupboards and every single nook and corner was filled with toys, games and comics, everything that young boys could dream of. Both of us were so overwhelmed by this display of loving affection, this eagerness to wipe off all our accumulated pain, that **we could do no more than just close our eyes and let it all sink in.**

Later on, I had the opportunity of discussing this entire home-coming with Mamoni, and asked her how much of a role she had in planning the event. She confessed that it was completely Kaku's baby, from conception to execution. She also told me that although the relationship between the two of them had taken seed about four years back, this was the day that she really fell in love with him. This was the day that mutual attraction got strengthened manifold with a layer of respect and gratitude, with a commitment that no challenge could ever hope to weaken.

Chotloo – Being a petit mal patient (Jul 1972)

Life in Hyderabad was good, just about perfect. There was, however, one fly in the ointment. Either due to the trauma of my parents splitting up, or more likely due to Baba being Rh positive and Mamoni being Rh negative, I had developed an ailment that I could not understand for a long time.

Sometime in our days at Calcutta during the 1969 to 1972 period, there suddenly started instances of my brain losing control over my central nervous system, albeit for short durations. My body would then go on doing exactly the same thing that it was doing before this episode occurred. If I was walking, I would continue walking, but without my eyes seeing or mind registering anything. Typically, each episode would last for about five to ten seconds, and then I would come back to my normal senses, the return being usually accompanied by an involuntary rubbing of my nose with my fingers. The frequency of these episodes varied from eight to ten times on a bad day to as low as once in two to three days during good phases, depending on factors such as ambient temperature, degree of exhaustion and mental stress, basically factors that caused hyperventilation.

Apart from the dangers associated with these temporary blackouts, as I like to call them, there was one rather embarrassing side effect. It often led to urinary incontinence; I would pee in my pants. If these episodes occurred at home or while playing with my dear friends in College Park, it would be easy to cover up through a quick change of clothes. In school, it was a different matter altogether. The evidence of the attack would be visible to all and sundry for quite some time, regardless of how much I tried to cover it with books and bags.

As word got around, I became a rather easy and popular target for boys seeking cheap thrills; it was only some of the most sensitive souls in my class who understood what I was going through and often shielded me from these harsh pinpricks. I don't blame them at all; after all, they were just young fun-loving boys who knew little about things like blackouts and petit mal.

Yes, petit mal is what I was diagnosed with. Petit mal literally means small illness in French, with grand mal meaning big illness. Later on, when I read Arthur Hailey's The Final Diagnosis (an informative novel, which I recommend to my readers, especially those with even the slightest interest in medical sciences), I gained an understanding of the genesis of this illness. It is often the result if one parent is Rh positive and the other is Rh negative, due to generation of antibodies in the mother's womb which go on to attack the nervous system of the unborn child.

I also learnt that by the time I was conceived, a test had already been discovered, Coombs Test, that could identify cases where the foetus was in danger of being harmed and hence, necessary precautions could be taken. Unfortunately, the progress of medical science in the West was not matched in India during the early sixties; Baby and I suffered as a consequence (Baby suffered from grand mal, being the classical progression from petit mal to grand mal to still birth, for successive children of parents having mismatched Rhesus factors).

Anyway, this was something that I had to live with, unpleasant as it was. For a while, I was prescribed a drug, Gardenal, that did reduce the frequency of the petit mal attacks. However, I soon realized that this was accompanied by a marked slowing down, or dumbing down, of my mental faculties. Reaction times were getting longer and I was definitely taking more time to assimilate knowledge; something that I was not prepared to accept. Without informing anybody, reckless as it may have been, I gradually scaled down the frequency of this medication and soon, I was back to my normal self. Quick on the uptake, as I have always prided myself on, but yes, occasionally wetting my pants and being the general butt of ridicule.

I lived with this rather embarrassing ailment all the way till April 2002. As this was identified to be an unacceptable risk for my bypass surgery, remedial measures had to be taken. A new drug had come into the market, Valporin, that treated the problem without it having the undesirable side effect of slowing down my reflexes.

It was a divine intervention for me, one that changed my life by removing many restrictions that were then in place e.g. driving, swimming, climbing heights etc. Looking back, it is quite likely that had I remained under continued medical supervision, I could have been rid of this disease quite some time back.

Life is indeed, full of strange ifs and buts.

Mamoni – Pawning jewelry (Jul 1974)

She has always been a special person. Regardless of her temper occasionally flaring out of control, or her tendency to boss around, there can be nobody like her.

When she was just a young mother of two, living in a state of extreme hand-to-mouth existence, both Igloo and Bigloo came down with bad cases of typhoid at the same time. Then, much more than now, typhoid was not good news for young children; doctors were more than a little worried about their prognosis. They needed a steady supply of fat-free protein that could be got only from spring chickens.

Dadu flatly stated that the limited family budget could not support the cost of two spring chickens every day, and Baba could add nothing further. So, what did Mamoni do? She did what any other superhuman and impossibly loving mother would do. Unflinchingly, she sold two gold bangles, out of her rather limited stock of jewelry and arranged for two spring chickens to be delivered every day to our doorstep.

Slowly but steadily, the boys recovered. Without this timely and selfless act from her side, which many then called unduly excessive and dramatic, we may have lost a brother or two. This would have been labeled a tragedy, gradually to be forgotten.

More recently, when we were in Hyderabad and the going was good, Kaku and Mamoni had a neat arrangement between themselves. He would take care of the fixed monthly expenses like rent, taxes, school fees etc. while she looked after day-to-day expenses like grocery, electricity, sightseeing and the like. The fare on our dining table was often a reflection of the number of patients she had attended to, in her Punjagutta clinic the previous day. It was strange, funny but true.

She knew how much Baby and I loved having our special Sunday breakfasts, with a typical spread including eggs to order, toast, milk, sausages, ham and fried tomatoes. Sandy Aunty used to comment "Jharna, you run a restaurant, not a home". On most Sundays, she would have enough in her handbag, but occasionally, Fridays and Saturdays were a little dry. After all, the need of patients to visit their doctor was not exactly determined by the appetite of her teenage boys.

On these days, when her kids were hankering for sausage and her handbag was light, what could be done? For Mamoni, the answer was simple.

Unthinkable for anybody else, she would take off her wristwatch, call Saraswati, her Lady Friday in the clinic and at home, and give her the shopping list along with the wristwatch. Saraswati, without being told, would go down to the local pawnshop, pawn the watch and with the cash obtained, get the required foodstuff from Sabon, the local grocery shop. The dining table would then take on its familiar fragrances and her kids would be all smiles.

Within a couple of days, as the handbag filled itself, Saraswati would make another trip to the pawnshop to redeem the watch. It was a well-oiled operation, as logical to

Mamoni as senseless as it was to anybody else watching from the sidelines. This was Mamoni.

Can you think of anybody like her, a leading doctor, pawning her wristwatch on a regular basis, just to arrange for her kids' favourite breakfast?

When God made you, dear Mamoni, he must have dropped the mould.

Suki – A quiet Diwali evening (Oct 1975)

In College Park, one of the most charming characteristics was the strong community bonding that we had between the four families who stayed there. Between the four couples and about half a dozen children, it always felt like we were a single joint family rather than four families living in a gated compound. This feeling of oneness would come to the fore particularly during festivals such as Holi and Diwali.

It was the Diwali of 1975, if I am not mistaken. As was the longstanding tradition, all the families had pooled in their stock of firecrackers, rockets and sparklers in readiness for darkness to descend. Once the sun went down and the diyas were lit, dressed in our Diwali finery, we congregated at the open space between the houses and started warming up to the sounds and lights of various firecrackers.

Suddenly, a firecracker that Mamoni was holding in her hand, the type that emits coloured lights from one end while you hold the other, burst and her palm was scalded. Immediately after cold water was applied, a bandage was tied but she was in a state of mild shock and in no mood to continue with the group festivities. She retired to our place, while the Diwali party carried on.

But, hold on!

There was this little nine-year-old girl, who also withdrew from the fun and frolic and quietly made her way to where Mamoni was sitting, all by herself. It was Suki. Seeing her approach, Mamoni asked her to go back to where the fun and games were in full swing, but the little girl would have none of that. She said "It's all right, Jharna Aunty, I would rather sit here with you, if you don't mind", displaying a sensitivity and sense of compassion that should have been way beyond her years. And sit she did, for no less than three hours, intermittently chatting with Mamoni or just being comfortable with silence when it crept in between their conversation.

I am not sure, but I think that it was at this moment, she became the apple of Mamoni's eyes, and marked herself as somebody out of the ordinary, somebody very special indeed. In so far as I was concerned, this was definitely the day a special part of my heart was reserved for her, in respect, for a nine-year-old child.

That's also the day I realized that **respect is not a function of age, it is but a reflection of your deeds.**

Dr. Vijay Kelkar – A chance meeting (Aug 1976)

Strange is life, often stranger than fiction.

Towards the end of my school days, when we were all in the midst of our final preparations for the Senior Cambridge exams, we had a visitor in our house for dinner, the renowned economist, Dr. Vijay Kelkar. After the dishes were cleared, my parents started to discuss various issues with him, with young me sitting on the sidelines, eagerly trying to soak in their thoughts on a wide range of topics. Somehow, the discussions drifted towards a totally new subject, economics.

Soon thereafter, it was easy, even for my untrained mind, to understand that this was not just a post-dinner conversation piece for Dr. Kelkar, it was something that inflamed and impassioned his very being. When he spoke of resource allocation being at the heart of economic development, of the need for well-structured schemes aimed at poverty alleviation, or of leakages in the system that create a huge disconnect between donors and recipients, it struck a chord in me. Something within me just cried "What can you do to help make this happen? Beyond being an armchair critic and attending seminars, how can you make a difference?"

Being deeply touched by the words of Dr. Kelkar and his passion about the subject called economics, I was now on the verge of giving up career options in science, be it engineering or medicine, for the wonderful world of economic policies, gross domestic product and consumer behaviour, even though I was a more than reasonably good science student, as my marks will testify.

Noting my more than passing interest, Kaku took me aside at this point and laid the cards down on the table as only he could, clearly and succinctly. He made it clear that once you gain entry to a reputed engineering school, you are more or less set up for life. Whether you excel or not, a comfortable life, with all its trappings, are virtually assured.

On the other hand, should you opt for economics, life will be good only if you graduate at, or near, the top of your class. Only then, will the doors to places like the famed Indian Institutes of Management (those days, there were only three IIMs at Ahmedabad, Bangalore and Calcutta), Xavier Labour Relations Institute or Jamnalal Bajaj Institute and career options through the Indian Economic Service open up.

As he underlined, engineering was a time-tested option that may or may not be emotionally rewarding in the long run. Economics, on the other hand, would open up far fewer options, where just being good would never be good enough.

I did not realize it then, but these couple of hours changed my life forever.

Man plans and proposes; God takes you down an unexpected fork in the road.

Chotloo – Senior Cambridge (Nov 1976)

The incident that I will recount here cannot be called just that; it was an epic.

For the Senior Cambridge finals, I had prepared two questions from Shakespeare's Romeo & Juliet, the Balcony Scene and Queen Mab's soliloquy, as well as could be done. Our English teacher, Mrs. Lalitha Christian (*whose naughty antics on a testerestone-charged group of teenagers led to half the class, including me, having a serious crush on her, but that is another story altogether*) had said that if either of these questions appeared in the question paper, I should just dive into them and great grades would be a given.

Guess what? Not one, but both the questions were present, in their full glory. I could not believe my luck. Words flowed from my pen to the answer sheet so fast that my fingers struggled to keep pace with my mind. My heart was racing, visualizing the amazing numbers that I would be gloating over once the results were out. In my state of unbridled euphoria, I finished the paper well ahead of time and handed it over to the invigilator. To be fair, he did raise his eyebrows wondering what had got over me to rush out of the examination hall in such an unseemly hurry, and wait for my friends to come out. I was eagerly waiting to share my good fortune with them.

After a while, it was Syed Akbaruddin, my dear quizzing partner, who came out and asked me how I fared. Naturally, I conveyed my elation to him in no uncertain terms and looked forward to his congratulatory hug. To my utter surprise, he blankly looked at me and asked "You answered both the questions?" It was now my turn to be totally perplexed. "What do you mean?" said I. Haltingly, Akbar drew my attention to the question paper and asked again "Did you not see that you were supposed to answer either one of them and four others?"

In my haste and delight, I had answered both of them and only three others. I looked at the question paper and, I exaggerate not a bit, felt my blood turn to icy cold water. I dashed to the exam hall as there was still some time left, maybe ten minutes or so, and pleaded, begged, cajoled, implored and beseeched the invigilator to give me a few minutes, to allow me to start another answer, but no mercy was forthcoming; no quarter was given.

I would gladly have traded places with Braveheart William Wallace; **being hung, drawn and quartered could not be a fate worse than what I was enduring then!**

Baby & Chotloo – Getting close to lions (Dec 1976)

During our stay in Hyderabad, picnics were commonplace. Sometimes, they took the shape of us College Park kids packing a few sandwiches and fruit juice in our hampers and taking off in our bicycles across the hills and vales of Banjara Hills. On other days, they were elaborate corporate affairs complete with liveried waiters, kebabs, fermented hops, song and dance. The common denominator was that everybody let their hair down and had unbridled fun.

In the winter of 1976, ASCI organized a picnic in a place called Gandipet, an amazing picnic spot. On one side, you had the huge Gandipet tank that served as the giant water reservoir for the twin cities of Hyderabad and Secunderabad. On the other side, you had the beautifully landscaped Hyderabad Zoo, in which the animals were not confined in constricted cages but were allowed to roam around in an environment that was as close to their natural habitat as possible.

Next to the zoo, work was nearing completion for the futuristic Lion Safari Park, where human visitors would be locked in cages while the lions prowled all around them, wondering how to get at the tasty contents of the grilled vehicles.

Coming back to the picnic, the event of the day. It was kicked off with the usual fare of morning snacks, outdoor games including badminton and cricket while some of the ladies oversaw the preparation of the delicacies that would adorn the lunch table. After a couple of hours, food was ready, as were the stomachs. In next to no time, we devoured the food, washed down with beer and cold drinks. Many of the not so younger members started adopting postures that were distinctly horizontal, allowing the food to settle down in a leisurely manner.

During this lull in proceedings, Baby and I decided to go for a stroll; to take in the eye-catching sights. After a while, we came across a dam-like structure, on top of which was a walking area that was quite wide. On to it, we climbed and started exploring the surrounding areas. On one side of the dam was the large expanse of the Gandipet lake; on the other were verdant forests, tall trees and colourful shrubs.

Suddenly, we noticed that we were at quite a height. This was not apparent on one side as the bountiful monsoon had raised the water levels in the tank. On the other side, there was a steep drop to the ground below, more than fifty feet, I guess. It was now time to get back and we turned for our return journey.

Wait a minute, what were those furry creatures down below, looking like some of the big cats in the jungle? Surely, they could not be what they looked like, like lions, could they? They could and did look like lions, because they were lions. Once this realization dawned on us, we simply froze.

The safety provided by the width of the dam suddenly became grossly inadequate. It was as if the dam was not wide enough for us to walk the distance from here to the picnic spot without slipping over one of the sides. We feared that we were headed either to the depths of the Gandipet lake or the jungle below where the lions appeared to be building up a healthy appetite for a couple of young Bengali lads.

For a couple of minutes, we stopped in our tracks; time stood still. Invoking all the mental strength, courage and the divine support that we could muster, we started moving forward, at a snail's pace. The dam was wide enough for us to casually walk across, but this was no ordinary stroll in the park. This was after all, the Lion Safari Park. Every couple of steps we looked down to the jungle, and there were the lions menacingly prowling all over the place.

After what seemed like an eternity, we reached the picnic spot and suddenly, the dam, the lake and the forest looked just as innocent and inviting as they did when we started our leisurely walk. Relief coursed through our veins filling us in a big rush.

Lions are the kings of the jungle, and I love everything about them. However, **this was a close encounter of a kind that I would rather like to pass on.**

Baby – Swimming pool drama (Oct 1977)

Having decided to move from Hyderabad to Calcutta, we planned to drive down after having sent our heavy luggage onwards by train. Although the road trip could be done in two days, we decided to take a couple of breaks on the way at

Vizag (where Kaku's brother used to stay along with his wife, Jethima, and his teenage daughter, Shoma) and Puri (to enjoy the sea beach, crabs and jumbo prawns for a day).

The distance from Hyderabad to Vizag being a little more than six hundred kilometres, we knew that it would be a long day on the road but given an early start, we hoped to reach Jethu's place in time for dinner. However, as things often do, our start was delayed by emotional farewells and then, the lunch break was extended as Kaku needed to rest. By the time we rang the bell on their door, everybody was fast asleep as it was past midnight. Finally, we did get in and crashed for the night.

Next morning, it was decided that we would spend an extra day at Vizag. This would not only give us a chance to spend some quality 'getting to know each other' time with Kaku's brother and his family, it would also give Kaku one more day of rest before we resumed the drive to Calcutta. While the elders lazed over beer and snacks at home, Baby, Shoma and I headed to Vizag Club for a swim and sandwiches.

Once at the club, Shoma and I got into the pool and started enjoying the water, sometimes swimming, sometimes splashing but always chatting and having fun. This was the first time that we were meeting her, and we were keen to get to know each other. This was taking place with two of us in the pool while Baby was strolling on the sidewalk, as he did not know how to swim.

All of a sudden, when I was near the deep end of the pool, Baby decided to play the fool, in a way that nobody could have expected. He jumped on my back, dressed in his T-shirt and shorts, without any warning whatsoever. Once he hit the water, his senses returned and now, it was his turn to panic. He realized the grave danger that he was in, and felt that clinging on to me was the only way out of this mess.

Unfortunately, this required him to put his arms around my hands, as tightly as he could. Hence, I was not being able to swim and both of us were now on the verge of going down under quickly, unless something could be done. Till date, I do not know how this brainwave struck me. It must have been the Almighty who had been taking care of us; there can be no other explanation. Stretching my hands and somehow sliding my arms out of Baby's grip, I reached out and pinched him as hard as I could, digging my nails as deeply as possible. He cried out loudly and for an instant, let go of my arms. This was enough for me to turn around and throw him towards the railings on the side, which he grabbed on to.

For a minute or so, both of us just kept staring at each other, without a word, without any expression. Then, I just let loose with my full stock of expletives, cursing his non-existent fossilized brain. Shoma, our cousin, who was blissfully unaware of what was happening, gave us this puzzled look that seemed to say "What on earth is wrong with you guys?" Once we explained to her the drama of the last few minutes, she joined in, blasting Baby out of sight. Not very ladylike, I seem to recall.

Just another swim in the pool. Turned out to be a touch more exciting, I would say.

Suki – Childhood queries (Nov 1977)

Earlier in this journal, I have talked about Suki, Sandy Aunty and Vijai. With their family, we shared a wonderfully inclusive relationship, the type that I would not have thought possible, especially in India, where people tend to be conservative in their outlook and hesitate to reach out beyond the bounds of their immediate family. Being six years older than Suki, and being reasonably well read and informed about various issues for my age, it was only natural that Suki and others often looked towards me for answers to questions that arose in their growing minds.

Towards the end of 1977, Suki and their family moved from College Park to their own house that was close, but not close enough to walk across every day. You had to catch a bus and then walk up the hill for a good thirty minutes to reach their place and thus, the frequency of my visits reduced to once a week, on Sunday mornings. This activity was carved in granite in my schedule and nothing could make me miss this weekly visit.

On one of these trips, I saw Suki, slightly pensive and withdrawn. This was not a usual sight, so I asked her what the matter was. She looked down towards her chest area and hesitatingly asked me, her Wikipedia of sorts, "Chotloo, do you think that I will get bumps?" A young girl of eleven asking a seventeen-year-old teenager this kind of question was as unexpected, as it was a badge of honour of sorts.

In that one moment, she revealed the faith she had in my knowledge, the kind of trust she had in me as a person that enabled her to ask such an intensely personal question to somebody who was neither a lady nor a family member. In truth, I felt honoured and elevated, if that's the right choice of words. Unhesitatingly, I responded "Sure, Suki, don't you worry. Give yourself a couple of years and you will surely get your bumps." Suki looked pleased and reassured.

On another occasion, confident that I had answers to virtually all questions, she came up to me and asked, without any warning of the salvo that she was about to fire "Chotloo, will periods be painful?" This one took me by surprise and even I, was not ready for this. Somehow, I regained my composure and spluttered "Suki dear, this is one question that I am totally not equipped to answer. This is something that you will need to ask Sandy Aunty."

I guess that even Encyclopedia Britannica has its own limitations.

Jadavpur University (JU) – The first few days (Sep 1978)

Triggered by a number of factors, mainly by the desire to stay with my family after Kaku joined Regional Computer Centre, Calcutta, I managed to get a 2nd year transfer to JU, something that was quite uncommon then as it is now. Towards the end of September, 1978, I cagily took my first steps in JU, and walked all the way to the 3rd floor of the Arts building that housed the highly respected Economics Department.

This was a place which I would formally be a part of, for not more than a year and a half, but where I formed friendships that would last for forty years, and more. Being a co-educational college, and that too being only my second exposure to spending quality time with the other fifty per cent of the universe, call them girls or ladies, it was somewhat unnerving for me. Not being sure of how to mix, interact and get friendly with them, let alone become friends with them.

Strangely enough, I realized that I was not alone. Our class was about fifty strong, and this apparent unease in how to mingle with the opposite gender seemed to be a common issue for everybody, regardless of the fact that all the other students had already spent a year and a half studying, chatting and socializing together.

The first thing that struck me as odd was that the class had two clearly demarcated halves; the girls sat on the left while the boys sat on the right. Nothing formal about it, but it was as formal as informal could possibly get, if you know what I mean. This did not go down well with my ideas of a mixed educational institution, having been brought up on Archie comics and the Secret Seven adventures. Where was the friendly banter and camaraderie between the boys and girls? Was JU a co-educational college only in name, with virtually two classes in one? Where East was East and West was West, never the twain shall meet, a la Rudyard Kipling?

This was not an acceptable situation, at least not for me. Along with some of my friends and friendly acquaintances (I use the word 'friend' with a lot of care and very selectively, as friends mean a lot to me, as I hope that I do to them), one fine morning we casually strolled over to the left side of the room, the 'girls' section' if you please, and took our places in the last row.

The collective gasp of shocked surprise rang across boys and girls alike, and reached even the furrowed eyebrows of our professors. It just could not be done, was the unanimous, if unspoken view.

Except, nobody told us that, and we were too dumb to understand. Well, not really.

Chotloo – Turning down the first job offer (Apr 1981)

After the Part 2 exams leading to our Bachelor's degree were done and dusted, we had a fairly long break. While most of our classmates were getting ready for the Master's degree in either Jadavpur University (inertia) or Calcutta University (a step up in terms of academic prestige), a few amongst us started looking at various other options too.

Staying on the roadmap that Kaku had outlined for me during the course of that fateful evening when we met Dr. Kelkar, I started preparing in earnest for the Common Admission Test to the three IIMs (Ahmedabad, Bangalore and Calcutta), arguably the most difficult entrance exam that there was, given the prestige attached to these institutions.

Over a period of three months, from early September 1980 to the third week of December, I went through dozens of practice tests, timed tests and what have you, not to speak of trying to expand my English vocabulary and logical deduction skills through all the GMAT books that I could lay my hands on. After the CAT on 21st December, I felt exhausted and drained; but also satisfied that I had given it my best shot. The rest was now in the hands of the Almighty.

We had to wait for a couple of months till the list of candidates progressing to the next stage of selections, through group discussions and detailed interviews on your specialized subject, would be announced. Fortunately, during this intervening period, I came to know that Hindustan Computers Limited (HCL) had sold a few mini-computers to Ballarpur Paper Mills who now wanted to recruit a couple of computer programmers right away. To help them out, HCL agreed to conduct a training program on BASIC for people with no prior exposure to algorithms or flowcharts, leave alone any specific programming language such as BASIC, COBOL or Fortran.

Based on an aptitude test. I was selected to be part of a 25-strong batch, out of which the best performing students would ultimately be offered a job with Ballarpur Papers. Here, it would be amiss if I did not make a special mention of Mr. Anirban Mukherjee and Mrs. Mala Roy, who made the subjects of algorithms, flow charting and computer programming as enchanting and interesting as they did. Later on, Mr. Anirban Mukherjee also became my colleague in CESC when I realised what a wonderful person he is, apart from being an extremely capable teacher.

The pay in question was quite attractive (if I remember correctly, it was around Rs. 1,200 per month back then). After quite a rigorous eight-week course, I was thrilled to learn that

I had come out on top of the class, and the proud recipient of the first job offer. I was feeling right on top of the world.

Coming back home, I saw a brown envelope waiting for me on my study desk from IIM Calcutta. And one more from IIM Ahmedabad (I got a letter from IIM Bangalore too, but unfortunately, it was a regret letter). With barely controlled nervousness, I opened the letters and was delighted to know that both the institutes were offering me admission to their flagship two-year residential programs.

Between earning an MBA degree from IIM and a job at Ballarpur Industries, it was not much of a contest.

Sometimes, I wonder, how it would have been if I had actually moved to Ballarpur, to take up the job and built a career in software development, instead of the career selected through a chance meeting with Dr. Kelkar and his passion.

Borda comes home after 8 years (Feb 1982)

It all started off as it was a dream.

For 8 long years, we were without our eldest brother. That stupid, impulsive person, who chose to disturb our resurgent family fabric being swayed by his admittedly beautiful cousin, Loya and her two slinky brothers, Alok and Amit, not to mention the smooth-talking Nantu mama and his oh, so elegantly turned out wife, Ruth Aunty.

Personally speaking, I must confess that I felt quite betrayed, in a sense, by Borda. How could he have left his younger brothers at this delicate stage in their lives, when they were just about trying to regain their feet and getting to terms with a whole new world, without Baba, with Kaku, that bore little resemblance to the horrors of New Alipur or the laid back affluence of Digboi? As the Lord Ram, how could he have just gone away, leaving his dear Lakshman, Bharat and Shatrughan behind? Agreed, he was struggling to come to terms with the new family equations, but was it any easier for his little brothers?

Anyway, that was behind us and there was nothing that we could do about it.

We used to, at least I definitely did, think that Mamoni was simply crazy, absolutely bonkers, to think that she could go to London and like in the most far-fetched of Hindi movie yarns, actually locate her son without having the slightest clue of where he was, or what he was up to. Often, I used to think that this was just an excuse that she would come up with to visit her beloved city of London, walk down the Thames, shop at Harrods and all that goes with it. Kaku, having his numerous official trips to the West, would accommodate both London and Mamoni, splitting the business class ticket into 2 economy class tickets after being sweet talked into it by Mamoni. Baby and I would have to make do with the usual tourist trinkets of posters, T-shirts and ball point pens in fancy shapes and sizes.

How we did under-estimate the power of positive thinking, the unbelievable strength of a mother's love that can actually make miracles happen, especially if it is helped along the way by her absolute faith in Ma Kali. The shakti (power) of a mother is the stuff that creates a universe; how trivial is finding your son in a tiny megapolis called London, where he is but 1 in oh, so many millions, in comparison? It just pales into insignificance.

Coming back to the narrative, after one of her numerous trips to the city called London, or it may have been during the trip itself when she bumped into Borda at Wimpy's – Oh, the very memory of what it must have been like, raises goose pimples all over me, even as I punch these letters on the laptop – we heard the most incredible news. News that we could scarcely believe to be true. Borda had been found – ordering a large portion of chips, but no fish – due to pocket constraints.

How Mamoni's heart must have hemorrhaged that day, I can only imagine. Her favourite son, her first born, having to start a full working day with just a plate of starchy, over-fried carbohydrates when back home, her own kitchen and pantry overflowed with all the goodies that you could possibly imagine? Oh God! How it must have felt to be a mother in this impossible to bear situation!

To make things even better, shortly thereafter we came to know that he would be coming to India, to Calcutta, to our 4th floor flat at 323, Jodhpur Park. Just imagine. How the days went by, as we counted down the hours and minutes, I cannot even begin to describe. It was as if our whole world revolved around just this one event – Borda's return, Khokababu's protyaborton (a blockbuster Bengali movie that literally translates to "The Return of the Prodigal Son", if you like. From the domestic help, Mamoni's nursing home staff to my college friends – nobody was spared this earth-shaking event, preparing for it, getting all excited and totally charged up about it.

The day came. I may be wrong, but I think that it was on this trip that Mamoni, with her usual 'could not care less' attitude for rules and regulations, sweet talked and bullied, as required, the airport staff at Dum Dum airport. In the blinkof an eyelid, she had bulldozed her way right inside the Immigration section to hug her very heart at the earliest, way beyond the reach of normal mortals who had to wait at the Arrival Lounge for their loved ones to emerge from the door,

What I, in fact we, did not realise was the speed with which time flies when you are counting down time for his return flight. I know that cold logic will vigorously disagree with me, but I am sure that time does not move at a constant rate, definitely not at the rate of 1 second per second, as I like to say it myself. Time spent waiting for your Borda to walk back into your life, must have taken at least ten times as much as when you are actually trying to catch up on everything that you have missed, on all the hugs you lost during the intervening years.

When the time to go could be measured in days, rather than weeks, tears started welling up within me – in a totally uncharacteristic and emotionally unstable manner; one that was totally not befitting a mature young man pursuing his MBA program, preparing for life. So what? The heart often has a mind of its own, that just ignores the dictates of the other 'mind' when it so chooses.

Soon, too soon, it was time for us to make that dreaded trip back to the airport, in total silence, willing a traffic jam every inch of the way that just refused to materialise. One final set of hugs and tears, and then Borda was off.

However, when all was said and done, when the tears had been wiped away, we knew that our dear Borda, our Brother Ram, was back in our lives, back in our hearts, where he always belonged, does belong and will always belong.

Abhik – Morning does not show the day (May 1986)

When I look back, trying to relive some of the most memorable incidents that have added colour to my life, I cannot but go back to the summer of 1986. Club 9 was then in its initial days; incidentally, this group has been one of the most enduring relationships that I have been part of, with it now being a healthy and mature thirty-five-year-old entity.

If I remember correctly, three of our Club 9-members (Abhik, Anup and I) had gone over to a common friend's

(Dhiman Banerjee) house for an all-night program of tandoori roti and chicken chaap, washed down with gin & tonic, to be followed by a movie-watching binge on the video cassette player. Here, I must confess that in addition to the films you expect to be watched in a family environment, there were a few of a slightly different genre too. And therein, lay the main reason for organizing this get together in our bachelor friend's apartment, on a weekend. Totally wrong, I accept, but boys will be boys.

From late in the afternoon on Saturday to the evening of Sunday, we enjoyed the endless supply of delicious food, fermented juniper berries and movies of varying kinds. It was a total free-for-all, with everybody doing as they felt like. Somebody would be taking a nap, while someone else would be ripping apart chicken legs with delightful savagery. If somebody would be watching a movie, someone else would be curled up on the sofa browsing through a magazine. It was the kind of break that we loved, especially as we had a long and tough week leading into it.

On Sunday evening, it was finally time to call it a day and head back home. It was time to get back to the daily grind. The locality where we were, was Salt Lake. Today, this area is one of the most affluent areas in Calcutta. Back in 1986, this area was being developed with many roads still incomplete. From where we were, we could see the lights of the Eastern Bypass that would take us back to good old South Calcutta, but we just could not find a connecting road.

At last, we reached a marriage hall and saw a car pulling into a parking slot. Diffidently, we asked the person at the wheel if he was headed to South Calcutta, which he was. Relieved, we decided to wait for the guest to have his dinner, so that we could follow him all the way back to familiar territory. This meant a rather long wait, but it was the only option.

Incidentally, I forgot to mention that Abhik had got married a couple of weeks before this event. On the day that we were coming back after our weekend binge, he and his wife, Anuradha (Bubu) had been invited to her aunt's place for dinner, for the first time after their marriage. It was thus, quite a formal occasion for both of them. Unfortunately, thanks to us getting lost in Salt Lake and then having to wait for our travel guide while he feasted on mutton kosha and fish fries, it was past ten p.m. by the time we reached Bubu's house where Abhik was supposed to pick her up, no later than seven-thirty p.m.

Later on, I came to know that there were the expected fireworks before Abhik managed to pacify his newly wedded wife. As she had given up on the evening, she had taken off her finery and gone back to her casual clothes. Getting dressed for dinner and putting the jewelry back on, took some time.

In the meantime, the excesses of the weekend coupled with sheer exhaustion of a rather long drive took its toll on me. As Abhik and Bubu would be sitting in the front of the car, I thought that I could go to the back seat and take a short snooze. As the seat was not long enough, I decided to put my feet out of the window. The weather being hot and sultry, I also opened a couple of my shirt buttons before going off to slumber land, hoping to wake up when I would hear them approaching.

I had seriously underestimated the extent of my body's need for sleep. When they did come down, both of them were shocked to see this tall and somewhat fat lad, snoring away in full glory, with his feet sticking out of the rear window and his chest buttons opened. Just the perfect image of a Hindi movie villain, except that this was real life, not reel life. Bubu had just one question to ask of Abhik, "Who is this loafer, and what is he doing in your car?" I presume that Abhik would have mumbled a few words, but I am sure that they did not sound very convincing.

Over time, this couple became two of my closest friends; in fact, more family than friends. **They say that morning shows the day; in this case, I am so happy that this adage was proved wrong, at least occasionally.**

Family – If there be heaven on earth, this is it (Sep 1986)

It was the autumn of 1986. We were all excited as Borda, along with his Dutch girlfriend, Riette, would be coming over to Calcutta. During the Puja holidays, we planned to go to Kashmir, surely the paradise on earth, for a week or thereabouts.

All the members of the family pooled in their resources and based on available information, made the necessary plans and budgets. We realized that that our budget was going to be tight, as the touring party was quite large. There were eight of us (Mamoni, Kaku, we four brothers, Riette and Shampi – Baby's wife). As both wanted to see the 'real India', we decided to travel by sleeper class i.e. 3rd class as it was called before things needed to be politically correct. One reason for agreeing to this suggestion was that it freed up precious resources, read money, for the plans that we had for our stay in Kashmir. Mamoni assured us that she would take care of the rail tickets through her contacts in the booking office.

We planned to make Srinagar our base station throughout the stay in Kashmir, with us making day trips to Gulmarg, Pahelgaon and Sonemarg to visit these scenic destinations. On other days, we planned to take in the sights of Srinagar and go for rides in the shikaras (long boats) around the picturesque Dal Lake. We left some time that we could spend doing whatever took our fancy, just the way a leisurely holiday should be like.

The much-awaited evening arrived, and we reached Howrah station (the station that serves Calcutta and its twin city, Howrah) well in time, armed with our bags and tasty food. How boring a long train journey would be, without home-made delicacies; otherwise, all you could do was laze on the berths, read the same old magazines and gaze out through the windows to watch the changing landscape.

As soon as the train came in to the platform and the reservation lists were put up on the coaches, we started checking out one after the other. Strange, our names did not appear to be on any of the lists. Irritated at our inability to even find our names on the reservation lists, Mamoni lost her temper and asked us not to display this total lack of competence. Prodded by her not so gentle demeanour, we did the rounds a second time, taking much more care, but we still could not find our names.

Time was now running out; the train was about to leave. We managed to find the TTE (Travelling Ticket Examiner) and asked him why our names were not on any of the reservation lists. He took one look at our tickets and casually remarked "Oh! These are unreserved tickets. You will need to get into the unreserved compartments and fight for space as best as you can. These tickets permit you to get on to the train, but no berths have been reserved for you." Our jaws collectively fell to the ground, making a loud clatter that shook us to the core.

Changing our posture and tone immediately, we pleaded for mercy, as we had three ladies in our group, with one of them being a foreigner. What impression would she carry back home, of our great country? The arguments and pleas became increasingly desperate as the time of departure approached. Less with the strength of our pleas and more with help of monetary inducements, he allotted three berths to us, for the ladies. Finally, we were on the train, our financial resources being adversely impacted. Over the next forty-two hours, we shared the berths amongst ourselves to help everybody catch at least a few winks while others sat packed tighter than sardines. Somehow, we managed to survive till we reached Jammu.

At Jammu, we boarded a luxury bus that would take us to Srinagar. The ten-hour long drive was truly mesmeric. All the travails of our train journey were forgotten as we gazed upon the lush plains of Jammu before descending to the magical valley of Kashmir. No poet, no travelogue could ever do justice to the visual extravaganza that lay before our eyes; majestic chinar trees, snow-capped mountains with their jagged peaks, young children selling apples that matched the colour of their cheeks; it made us wonder if this could be part of the same planet in which we lived.

Reaching the central bus depot in Srinagar, we made enquiries and finalized a week-long deal with a houseboat owner. To reach the houseboat, we had to take a shikara ride across Dal Lake; our holiday had begun.

Just as we were about to pull into the jetty, we saw a group of young girls, admittedly pretty, on the houseboat next to ours. Borda could not resist this opportunity of impressing this bevy of local beauties. Without any warning, he stripped down to his bare essentials and jumped into the lake and started swimming.

The only hitch was that the sewage of all the houseboats is directly pumped into the Dal Lake and naturally, the water is not exactly the healthiest. This, Borda realized over the next twenty-four hours, as he parked his backside on the toilet, spewing out loose motions with a touch of blood, almost continuously. Still, it was a small price for being the hero. Right, Borda? Did you get any of their telephone numbers?

Over the next few days, we made a number of trips, as planned. If anything, the charm of each and every one of these places far exceeded even our wildest imagination. How could such insanely beautiful places exist? Is this a dream, or is it for real? Believe me when I say that just seeing these places convinces you that there has to be a supreme being, a divine force; who else can even imagine such grandiose beauty, leave alone putting it in place for us to see, touch and feel? If ever I had any doubts that God exists, they disappeared when first I lay my eyes on Kashmir.

During this period, we had experiences to fill a lifetime; some good, some excellent, and some which were not so pleasant. On the way back, we realized that going to Kashmir on a tight budget and having the time of your life do not go together. And yes, did I mention that we were all so taken in by the quality of dry fruits, saffron, kurtas and walnut wood carvings that we just had to take a few of them home?

Things got to a point that when we finally boarded the train at Jammu for Howrah, we had less than a hundred rupees (a little more than two dollars) to take care of the eating and drinking needs of eight adults over forty-two hours. This was in the days when plastic money had not yet surfaced; hence no credit was available.

How did we manage? We bought a bag of puffed rice, a large portion of peanuts and about a dozen bottles of drinking water. God alone knows how, but we managed to return to Howrah station, hungry, tired and disheveled. We did not even have money to pay the taxi for the journey from the railway station to our home; we needed to rely on our cook to bail us out on arrival.

This was a holiday that we will never forget; it gave us a glimpse of what Heaven is.

Family – A holiday to remember (Jan 1987)

Towards the end of January 1987, the calendar sprung a pleasant surprise on us. Thanks to the national holidays and weekends coming together, all offices would be closed for four consecutive days, Friday to Monday. After deliberating on how we could make the best use of this pleasant coincidence, we decided to go out of Calcutta for a totally impromptu trip to local places of interest, within a radius of around three hundred kilometres.

Huddled around the map, we decided on the following holiday plan:

Day 1: From Calcutta to Chandipur (sea resort), overnight stay at Chandipur

Day 2: From Chandipur to Simlipal (tiger reserve forest), overnight stay at Simlipal

Day 3: From Simlipal to Jhargram (heritage bungalow), overnight stay at Jhargram

Day 4: Jhargram to Gadhiara (confluence of Damodar and Rupnarayan) to Calcutta

All of us got busy in making the necessary arrangements; luchi, aloor dum, egg curry, cards, music cassettes, checking the tyre pressure, mobile oil, brake fluids etc. The excitement was truly palpable as this was going to be the first major outing for the family (except Borda, who had already moved to UK) after quite some time, apart from our trip to Kashmir the previous year (another holiday that is difficult to forget, more of that elsewhere).

Incidentally, the thought of making reservations at the hotels and guest houses where we planned our night halts and visits never occurred to us. After all, we were the polished and suave city travelers. Surely, the semi-urban places we were planning to honour with our presence would not dare to insist on trivialities such as advance bookings and permits. Would they, could they?

On the 23rd morning, we packed ourselves into our ever-reliable car, the royal blue WME 8413. Of course, this was preceded by the usual jostling about which of the brothers would get to be squashed in the middle of the rear seat; I do not remember who won this unenviable privilege.

Making the customary breaks along the way, for leisurely cups of tea, an occasional mishti, daab (green coconuts) and lunch, we reached Chandipur around 6 p.m. We were tired, cramped and eager to stretch our legs in the comfort of the rooms.

Rude shock number 1 awaited us.

The place where we went to, Pantho Nibas, was fully booked (apparently, we weren't the only family to have hit upon the brilliant idea of going around the country side to take advantage of the long break). To make things worse, there was no other place to stay in for the night, that was even remotely comfortable and respectable, especially as we had a lady in our midst. After a lot of cajoling, pleading and deploying the final and failsafe ploy of a generous tip, the manager agreed to open the bar of the resort for us, but only after closing hours.

Since we had some time to kill, we trooped out to the beach and relaxed, soaking in the sand, the sea breeze and the sounds of the ocean. Back to our makeshift bedroom, the bar area, we convinced the resort manager to whip up rice, chicken curry and dal for dinner before lying down on the floor to get some sleep.

We brothers were too excited to sleep for long. Being city slickers, the call of the sea, and that too at a few minutes walking distance, was too much for us to resist. Early in the pre-dawn period, when even the earliest bird had not yet left its nest, the three of us snuck out of bed and trotted down to the beach. Where, the strangest of sights awaited us. The sea had vanished. It had, just gone.

Only a few hours back, the majestic Bay of Bengal roared at metronomic intervals and its waves constantly threatened to wet our feet. And now, it was nowhere to be seen. If it was just me, I would have thought that I was hallucinating. But, could all of us be hallucinating together, with exactly the same vision?

No, that was surely not possible. After a bit of soul searching and looking suitably puzzled, it dawned upon us that this was the naughty moon at work, exerting lunar gravitational forces that resulted in jwar (high tide) and bhata (low tide) on the sea. The sea floor in the area being flat, even a slight reduction in the water levels would cause the sea to recede by us much as two kilometres from the shore.

Thrilled, we walked in to the sea as far as we could, picking up sea shells as they caught our fancy. After a while, we heard the local folk yelling out to those taking an early morning stroll on the wet sands, to return to the safety of the beach. As the sea recedes quickly when the water level falls, it comes back just as fast when the levels rise. We scampered back and proceeded to have a hearty breakfast, excited by what we had just seen and learnt. Truly, it was quite an unforgettable morning.

Chandipur episode being over, now it was time to move to Simlipal, the tiger reserve forest which was about a hundred and twenty kilometres away. After a pleasant drive through green woods and tall trees, we reached the gates of Simlipal Forest Reserve around lunch time, where a smiling Forest Officer politely asked to see the permit (to go inside the forest) and reservation slip (for the guest house where we planned to spend the night in). We were taken aback by his strange requests, for entry permits and reservation slips. Surely, that could be managed through the usual combination of cajoling, pleading and wallet warming. Right?

Wrong. The forest officer insisted that no permit, no entry. No reservation slip, no stay at the guest house. Stubbornly ignoring the presence of the lady in our group and our pleas of helplessness, he stuck to his guns. Incidentally, he did have one casually hanging by his side. This was the end of our visit to Simlipal, along with our dreams of a possible sighting of the majestic cats in the wild. Disheartened, we decided to move on to Jhargram, having no other option.

Now, we were quite unsure about what awaited us there, and Mamoni's legendary temper was beginning to make its presence felt. I suspect that had it not been for us brothers being in the car and our constant attempts to lighten the atmosphere ("What's the fun if everything goes like a pre-planned conducted tour? Where is the excitement?" etc.?), things could well have gone out of hand.

Late in the evening, we reached Jhargram and surprise, surprise, the same old routine had to be gone through, fortunately with better-than-expected results. We were given two spacious and well decorated rooms to relax in. This was topped off by a lavish dinner where the food was piping hot, deliciously cooked and served with grace and style. In short, a meal and a place to stay that matched our expectations, or to be more specific, that met Mamoni's definition of acceptable arrangements.

The next morning, we took a walk around the hotel; it was actually the home of the local zamindars that had been converted into a heritage hotel. We took in glimpses of rural life, with villagers going around their morning chores, ducks and geese strolling around the ponds, and yes, the beauty of the majestic sal trees that surrounded the place. What a gorgeous sight it was! It was then time to bid goodbye to Jhargram and get going on the way to our final stop, Gadhiara.

None of us had any idea regarding this place, except Kaku. He had been informed by his colleagues that there was this nice resort, worth going to for a day, that lay at the confluence of two of Bengal's mostmighty rivers, the beautiful Rupnarayan and the powerful Damodar. By the time, we approached Gadhiara, we were not quite sure of where the resort was. We kept asking people on the way and got conflicting directions. Later on, we discovered that the reason for this was simple; the resort was still under construction and hence, few had any clear idea of where it was and more importantly, how do you reach that place.

By now, it had become quite dark; we were exhausted and tempers were frayed. Not an ideal combination if you are looking to reach a place that is unknown to you and most people in the vicinity too. And, no GPS – we are talking of the late eighties. As the night became darker and menacing, we kept moving along, desperately hoping to see a signboard of sorts. We had no such luck. After a while, the road that we were on seemed to be on an upward climb. It also appeared to get narrower. Unfazed, we kept moving forward, towards our destination we hoped.

After some more time, we heard a strange sound on both sides of the car. The night had become pitch dark, being a moonless night and there was virtually no visibility behind us. The strange sound was quickly identified as being that of water lapping gently but ominously at the banks. The question in our minds was, how could this be heard on both sides of the car?

And then, in a dreadful Eureka moment, it struck us. To confirm or dispel this awful thought, that we dared not articulate, Kaku and Mamoni peered out from their windows, slowly and very carefully. Our worst fears were confirmed. We had somehow managed to climb on to an embankment that separated the two rivers. The embankment was just wide enough for a car to pass, but one, not two; turning around was not an option. Everybody broke out into a cold sweat. Were we now heading for a watery grave?

We kept moving forward, invoking the blessings of all the divine forces we knew, as the embankment continued to shrink in size. We came to a point where a bridge could be seen, but clearly, it had left its better days way behind. Kaku knew that there was only a slight chance of it being able to support the weight of the car, but definitely not with the full payload of four passengers and the driver.

Having no choice, we got down from the car, and in small and measured steps, walked across the bridge. Once we were safely on the other side, Kaku revved up the engine to full power and then, just let go. In an instant, the car roared to life and jumped over the rickety bridge. Kaku got down, and puffed three cigarettes without a break, his hands and face clammy with sweat.

Such a close shave with disaster, we have not had ever before. Looking back, this was a holiday to remember, **not the least because it strengthened the ties of each and every one of us with the Almighty. Without His divine intervention, there was just no way that we could have seen it through.**

Suki – Meeting her after 12 years (Aug 1990)

After we left Hyderabad in 1978, fate kept me away from my dear friend, Suki, for twelve long years. In August 1990, the annual convention of Computer Society of India was held in the Garden City, Bangalore. As part of the delegation from CESC, it was my pleasant duty to attend the same. Those days, there was no direct flight from Calcutta to Bangalore; the only option was to go to Bangalore taking a short break at Hyderabad in between.

On the way back, there was a layover of around three and a half hours at Hyderabad. I don't know what came over me, but I suddenly checked in my baggage for the connecting flight to Calcutta, took my boarding pass and caught an auto for Road No. 12, Banjara Hills. Hyderabad is not one of those sleepy towns where change is measured in decades. Give this city a couple of years, and you will have difficulty in recognizing your own neighbourhood; this was a city on the move that was driven by its mission to catch up with tomorrow as fast as it could. I wish that I could say the same about my own city, the culturally rich Calcutta.

Anyway, having come to my favourite city after so long, I was struggling to see familiar landmarks. Where there were hills, shone large shopping complexes. Where there were lakes, stood luxurious five-star hotels. Areas, which were essentially residential in nature, had now become commercial hubs. To make things worse, I did not even remember the exact house number. All I knew was that Suki's house was near the top of the road, after the road went down. Not at all reassuring, was it? That is exactly how I felt, and the feeling got worse every time the auto rickshaw driver asked for increasingly specific directions.

God must have been on my side that afternoon, as I smelt and sniffed my way to their house, marked by a couple of false starts. When I finally saw the familiar gate to "SUVIMA", I could have leapt for joy.

Climbing up the stairs, I rang the bell and there in front of me, stood dear Sandy Aunty. "Chotloo!" she cried out loud. "What brings you here?" Hugging me tightly, she took me inside and in next to no time, we were racing across the years, catching up with each other, not caring that more than a decade had passed after we had met. After a while, I asked about Suki and was told that she had to go for her rounds at the hospital where she was working, but was expected to be back any time now.

Sipping our cups of tea, reminiscing over old times, my eyes kept shuttling between my wrist watch and the main door, hoping that Suki would walk in through that in time for us to meet. Delaying my departure to the extent possible, I was desperately wishing her to come back home. Finally, I had to give up and returned to the airport, that was not too far away, but it wasn't too close either. Sort of an in-between distance really. The check-in formalities having been completed earlier, I sat down, quite disappointed at having come so close to meeting my dear friend without actually doing so, and waited for the departure call.

Suddenly, I saw this young lady, peeping into the departure lounge, looking for something or someone. **Hesitantly, she came up to me and asked "Chotloo?" and I could have died with relief, with joy, just then and there.** She had come back home just after I left. Getting to know that I was on my way back to Calcutta but could be caught at the airport if she wanted to, she needed no second invitation. As fast as her Morris Minor would allow, she reached the airport and here we were.

Not knowing how to break the ice, admittedly a thin film, we ordered coffee and sandwiches. We sat down on the balcony overlooking the tarmac, so that I could keep an eye on the aircrafts arriving and departing, and spend as much time as possible with Suki. God knows how time flew, as we bombarded each other with endless questions and answers, trying to collapse a decade full of inputs and outputs into the few minutes that we had at our disposal.

After a while, it struck me that a particular aircraft appeared to be stationary on the tarmac for quite some time. Strange, wasn't it, I asked Suki. She agreed, only for both of us to hear "This is the final call for Mr. Debasish Ghosh, passenger travelling to Calcutta on flight ...." I jumped up, gave Suki a big hug, and ran to the aircraft. As soon as I got inside, I could feel the dirty looks of more than a hundred passengers boring into me in sheer disgust. After all, they had been detained for more than half an hour, while Suki and I were sipping our coffee and munching on shared memories.

It was a layover like no other, one that will stay in my mind forever.

Mamoni & Kaku – Being torn between 2 boats (Aug 1992)

Mamoni, Kaku and Baby moved from Hyderabad to Calcutta, in late 1977. I rejoined the family a few months later, after completing the 1st year of my degree course in Nizam College, Hyderabad. Helped by Kaku's influence with the JU top honchos, I was admitted to the Economics Department as a 2nd year student.

Coming back to Calcutta also meant that I reconnected with my uncles, aunties and cousins on Baba's side in a big way. When we were based out of Hyderabad, Baby and I would spend our annual vacations at New Alipur, while Mamoni and Kaku would spend theirs at his home in North Calcutta. This was an arrangement that we reached within ourselves, as it would help us stay in touch with Baba's family.

Things changed when we moved to Calcutta on a permanent basis. The way I saw it, whatever happened between Mamoni, Baba and Kaku was something that concerned only them, and related only to them. There was no reason why any issues that they may have had should cast shadows on my relationship with my uncles and aunts, and most importantly, my cousins as we belonged to a different generation altogether. Apparently, this line of thinking went down well with the people at New Alipur, but not so with Mamoni and Kaku.

I suspect that there may already have been an element of insecurity in Kaku's mind as other than Baby, none of us brothers had agreed to change our surname from Ghosh to Maitra. Secondly, my hero worship of Baba was all too evident for anybody to see, especially as I used to hold Kaku responsible for my parent's breakup (rather unfairly, as I can clearly understand now, but those days, I was not the most rational being and definitely not where Baba was concerned). Thirdly, being new to Calcutta and JU, New Alipur was a comfort zone as far as I was concerned as it meant being around people who I had spent a lot of time with.

Mamoni, being as intelligent and sensitive as she was, was quick to pick up on Kaku's insecurity, especially as far as I was concerned. Baby had amalgamated with the Maitra identity much faster, and to a much greater degree, than I had. Borda and Mejda were, to put it bluntly, a little beyond reach due to their advanced age and limited interaction with Kaku. I was the guy caught in the middle; the young boy whom Kaku had always seen as his son, but also the young rebel who refused to give up on his father's family.

This led to me having to play a balancing act all the time, especially on weekends when I would go over to New Alipur to spend my evenings chatting, playing cards or enjoying a meal together. Somehow, Mamoni and Kaku had the impression that the New Alipur wing of my family had a single point agenda of poisoning my mind against them, but nothing could have been further from the truth.

Whenever talk of Mamoni happened (Kaku was not discussed too often), it would always be about how loving and generous she was, of how one call from Baba across the hall would be enough to send Mamoni rushing to respond and similar anecdotes. It was mostly a time and place for pleasant memories to be recalled, to walk down memory lanes full of love and affection.

Back in Jodhpur Park, the environment would often be charged with tension. Ranging from a sullen silence at the dining table, to remarks such as "Chotloo, you cannot ride two boats at the same time; you need to choose between them", it was incredibly difficult for me to cope with this constant pressure.

There were times that I was tempted to just call it a day, to scale down my ties with New Alipur. I knew that if I did so, I would be swamped with expressions of affection, being but an outpouring of their relief that I belonged emotionally, only to Mamoni and Kaku. But then again, **it just was not right, according to my inner voice, and I continued to fight for my belief, difficult as it was proving to be.**

There would be times, as Mejda and Borda know well, that the pressure would become too much for me to bear. On a number of occasions, I, a thirty-year-old man, would burst into tears, seeking divine help. God, nobody should ever have to face this kind of situation, being forced to choose between one part of your family over another, or have your parents looking over your shoulder, trying to make sure that your loyalties do not shift.

In various shades, this conflict had to be faced by me for a long period of time, for the better part of twenty-five years. If the years between 1969 and 1972 was sheer hell, this period, while being nowhere as intensely painful, kept pricking me quite uncomfortably from time to time. The worst part of it was that it was so uncalled for, as Mamoni and Kaku were always going to be my first family, post-1972. **If only they had that unquestioning faith and confidence in me, and my love for them ...**

Tani –The unforgettable comeback (Mar 1993)

A lot of this journal has been written in a mood of serious introspection. Lest one gets the feeling that life has been one unbroken series of challenges and troubles, of gloom and doom, let me assure you that would be totally off the mark. Let me try and lighten the mood by recounting one of the funniest episodes that I can recall. With crystal clear clarity, even though it dates back to maybe thirty years ago.

As far as I can remember, it was Bubu's birthday. We had all gathered at Pipi's home for evening snacks and dinner. Sometime in between, the junior brigade, if you can call Tani and me to be part of that group, went over to the children's bedroom and started chatting amongst ourselves.

All of a sudden, the imp in me awoke and I had this irresistible urge to play a prank on Tani. Normally, she would be the one doing these things, putting me in spots that I would find difficult to wriggle out of. That day, I felt that it was payback time.

Taking out a matchbox from my pocket, I innocently asked "Tani, by any chance, would you happen to have a cigarette on you?" Hearing this, Bubu, Monai and Munmun (my three cousins) just stared at me, gaping open-mouthed. Didi-bhai

(Tani) a smoker, is that what I was implying? Could that really be? I just loved this moment, having put Tani in a corner after having waited for a long time to do so.

Refusing to be outsmarted, almost instantly, she retorted "Chotloo, would you, by any chance, be having a sanitary pad with you?" While this response totally knocked me out, never expecting Tani to come up with something as unmentionable as this, my three younger cousins just screamed at the same instant "Didi-bhai, how can you say something like this?", covered their mouths with their hands and just ran away from the room, leaving me in a state of utter shock.

My God! What was this girl made up of? Was there nothing off limits, out of bounds for her? That day, I learnt a lesson that I have never forgotten since.

Beware of this lady's retorts. They can hit you where you never expect it to.

Munmun – Seconds away from abduction (Oct 1993)

A time-honoured tradition in New Alipur was to have a family dinner on Ekadashi, the day after the last day of the Pujas. On this day, the youngsters would seek the blessings of their elders, and family members would embrace each other, wishing all the very best for the year ahead. This evening, in 1993, was planned to be one such day, with Pipi being the hostess. I joined in for the festivities, chit chat and to meet all my relatives from Baba's side.

After an elaborate dinner, as the night was winding down, I took my leave and got ready to return home, in Jodhpur Park. Munmun (Sujata Ghosh, Tani's youngest sister) also needed to get home quickly as she had a class test the next day, and requested me to drop her home before I headed out to Jodhpur Park.

Her house being only a short distance from Pipi's, we planned to walk it and thereafter, I would take a taxi to go home. It was around ten p.m. when we left Pipi's house and started on the short walk to Munmun's place. The road was dark, but that was of no concern, as we were familiar with both the road and the locality; what was more, many of our friends stayed there.

We crossed a small shop in front of which a few young men were sitting in their car, chatting amongst themselves and having a casual smoke. Midway through our walk, just as were passing in front of the house of one of our friends, a taxi overtook us. Rather strangely, a few young men peered out of it. We felt awkward, if not uncomfortable due to this, but didn't think much of it. Just after crossing us, the taxi stopped and four men got out and started walking in our direction.

Approaching us, they demanded to know who we were, why we were on the streets so late in the night, where we were going to, and so on. After hearing our curt replies, something triggered a totally unexpected response in the group as a whole. So perfectly coordinated were their subsequent actions that it had to have been planned all along. One of the guys asked Munmun to hand over her jewelry, which she was happy to, as she was wearing only junk jewelry rather than any serious gold or silver stuff. Not satisfied with this, two of the guys suddenly made a grab for her, while one guy came forward and held a country-made gun at my temple.

By this time, Munmun was screaming, "Chotloo-da, help me, hold me, don't let go of me". Somehow, I was just trying to hold on to her, but realized that it was a hopeless case of four against one, with me not exactly being Superman. To top it all off, there was this gun cocked against my head. At that point,

I had a sinking feeling that **it was just a question of time before** I would be overpowered, and **Munmun would be dragged off into the waiting taxi, for a fate that I shudder to articulate.**

At this moment, the car that we left behind a few minutes back came to life, and we saw a ray of hope. Strangely, the car just sped past us and our hearts sank. The house in front of which all this action was taking place, also shut its windows; friends, huh?

But wonders never cease.

As we came to know later, the car that crossed us had gone to pick up a couple of other guys and returned to where we were. Seeing them return with reinforcements, our wannabe abductors quickly jumped into the taxi and took off at full speed. Although the guys in the car gave chase, the taxi got on to a busy road. By the time it was caught, the four men had disappeared into the crowd (it was immersion time for the idols and the roads were jam packed).

For a few minutes, Munmun and I just stood there, profusely thanking these guys who saved us from the unspeakable and unthinkable. Later, we trudged back to Pipi's place, where we had to recount the whole event. We also went to the local police station to lodge a formal complaint. As was only to be expected, nothing ever came out of it.

After all the formalities at the police station were complied with, I called Mejda and asked him to come and pick me up, as I was not in an ideal frame of mind to catch a taxi. When he did arrive, without asking any questions, Mejda assured me that he had brought a fair amount of cash, expecting that it would be required to pay bail and have me released for whatever crime that I may have committed. In spite of all that

I had just been through, I burst out laughing seeing the funny side of it all.

Baby – Shock departure (Oct 1994)

As any Calcutta resident will agree, Durga Puja is the one festival that we look forward to, regardless of caste, creed or gender. Within the four days celebrated as the Pujas, the most auspicious day of all is Maha Ashtami, the day for which we preserve the best of the very best, the most glittering of sarees and ornaments.

The year was 1994. After quite a few years, Mejda, Baby and I were together in Calcutta for the Pujas. A few days back, we had also a bought a new Ambassador car that we planned to do the rounds of the Puja pandals in, apart from visiting our favourite eating joints. On Maha Saptami (the evening before Maha Ashtami), the three brothers went out to stock up on a whole range of video cassettes; Hindi romance, English war movies, Hindi thrillers and a few naughty ones too (for our private viewing, when Mamoni and Kaku would be fast asleep). To keep our stomachs and mouths in good humour, we had also gone to our favourite delicatessen to purchase heaps of sausages, ham, salami and baked beans. In short, we were all set for a gala fun fest, the likes of which we had not had for a long time.

To make the day extra special, we had also invited seven couples of the Club 9 gang (Debashis & Pinky Roy, Biswajit & Tutu Nag Chowdhury, Anup & Bubun Ghosh, Abhik & Bubu Bhattacharya, Bapu & Tuli Sircar, Amitava & Indrani Shome and Gautam & Pappu Dasgupta) for a grand lunch together. As Sandip and Anita Dasgupta had relocated to Vadodara by then, we would be missing their presence.

Early on the morning of the big day, the matron-in-charge of JCMC, Bhanu-di, started knocking loudly on our main door and insisted that Mamoni go along with her as soon as possible. She was looking agitated, and this worried Mamoni. In turn, she woke Kaku up while our cook, Nikhil, woke Mejda and me up.

When we asked the matron what the matter was, what was so urgent that made her come so early in the morning, she replied that Baby was not looking good and that we needed to go to the nursing home without any delay. Within a few moments, we rushed over and Mamoni practically ran from the car to the nursing home, to the operation theatre where Baby was lying, apparently in deep sleep, as an untrained eye would see.

Not to Mamoni and her practiced eyes. "Oh! My God! He has gone!" she exclaimed and just collapsed on to a nearby chair. Unbelievingly, Kaku, Mejda and I went in and

there, in a perfect sleeping posture, lay our little darling brother, in eternal sleep,

completely at peace, as peaceful as he had never been in his whole life. The give-away froth trickled down his nostrils, but apart from that, there was nothing to indicate that anything was out of the ordinary.

For me, it was just too much to take. Somehow, I stumbled out of the nursing home and made my way to Abhik's house and rang the bell. It was six-forty-five in the morning when I walked up the stairs and just about managed to find my way to a chair. Abhik took one look at me and knew that something was wrong, terribly wrong. He asked me what had happened, wondering if something had happened to Mamoni or Kaku.

When I mumbled "Baby", he could not believe his ears. How could anybody? Baby, the young prince of our household, was barely thirty years old and his entire life lay waiting to be lived. How could he possibly leave us forever, especially when just the previous day had been spent in so much gaiety, excitement and joy?

Anyway, practical sense soon overcame Abhik, and he calmly pointed out that we had a long day ahead of us, and I should eat a couple of sweets to give me energy. Rather incongruously, I requested Abhik to please inform the Club 9 members that the get together was called off; funny, how these trivial things come to your mind at times like this. After this was done, Abhik and I walked to JCMC where the rest of my family was still trying desperately to come to terms with what had just happened.

It was mentioned that we would need to get an autopsy done, as it was an unnatural death. At this point, Mamoni stepped in decisively, as she often has, when circumstances require her to do so. She clearly stated that there would be no autopsy; there would be no more cutting up of her dear son's mortal remains. He would go on his final journey as handsome as ever, with no disfiguration whatsoever.

To ensure this, she, the mother of her thirty-year-old boy, wrote the necessary death certificate and proceeded to the crematorium and calmly waited for the final rites to be completed. I remember Kaku crying like a baby, Mamoni maintaining a stony exterior with Mejda and I totally bewildered at the sudden turn of events.

Shortly after we came back home, after immersing Baby's remains in the Ganges and having our cleansing bath, there were all our friends from the Club 9 group, in full force, quietly hanging their heads down in collective grief, taking turns to console us. What was planned to be an afternoon of fun and frolic, of games, good food and gaiety had been turned on its head. Disbelief, coupled with a total lack of comprehension, was evident on everybody's face.

A fall out of Baby leaving us this way, was the sheer terror I felt, every day, for quite some time after this, especially when returning home from anywhere; be it office, the market place or a friend's home. This would be exacerbated if I happened to see even a couple of cars parked at our doorstep, making me wonder if somebody else had decided to leave us now.

Till this day, we do not really know what happened on that fateful morning. Was it a case of accidentally overdosing on nitrous oxide, as Baby did like to take a whiff to help him go to sleep in the comfort of an air-conditioned operation theatre? Was he so destroyed mentally having seen his dear Shampi cradling her new-born child in Garden Apartments that he decided that life was just not worth living? Or was there some foul play that he was unwittingly a witness to, for which he had to be silenced?

The answer, my friend, is blowing in the wind, as Bob Dylan would say.

Chotloo – Introspection (Dec 1999)

When I was hospitalized in late 1999, following a rather serious heart attack, unexpectedly I got a chance to think a lot of who I am, what I should be doing, and if I should be changing some basic equations in and around my life. Somewhere in the day-to-day hustle and bustle of everyday life, these important, but not urgent, issues had got swept under the carpet for far too long. Something had to be done, some serious re-evaluation needed to be carried out.

Being a patient in the ICCU wing, the hospital had issued only two visiting cards to my family, one to Mamoni and the other to Koli. As there were many others including Kaku, Borda and Mejda who wanted to visit me; Koli was asked to give up her card. While I did not understand the full significance during the early days of my convalescence, later I realized that this was just not right. **As my wife, Koli's right to the visiting card could not be equated with anybody else; to take the card away from her was to diminish her position in a way that was totally unacceptable.** Would something similar have happened if Borda or Kaku was hospitalized? Would anybody have even dared to take the visiting card from Boudi or Mamoni? If that was inconceivable, then why was Koli singled out for this grossly unfair behaviour?

The second issue that occupied my mind during this period was a strong realization of how I needed to re-arrange my priorities, and the way that I would face life going forward, regardless of its duration. For too long, I had developed stoicism, bordering on passivity, to an extent that it seemed like second nature to absorb what people or situations threw at me, not fighting back, not indulging in tit for tat.

Perhaps, it was because I felt that it was the right thing to do, perhaps it was caused by a need to be supported and hence, avoid conflict regardless of consequences. This, I realized, had to stop, this had to change. **As a husband and a father, my primary responsibility was towards Aditi and Anushka, and nothing and nobody could ever again be allowed to take precedence.** This was not an easy stance to take, as my earlier persona was so different, so accepting and adjusting.

The third issue, while being less serious, was just as disturbing to me. Initially, Anushka was told that I was away for a couple of days on work but later on, it was explained to her that I was not well and had to be hospitalized. She was just four years old when this happened but she insisted on coming over to see me.

When she arrived at the hospital, the first thing that struck her was the strange dress that her father was wearing, a drab blue cross-checked gown, tied together at the waist with a knot, a far cry from the smart outfits that she was used to seeing. The plaintive question in her eyes and asked by her voice "Why on earth are you dressed like this?" pierced my soul. To the extent, that on the day that I was discharged, I specifically asked to be given early notice of her arrival so that I could be in my normal office dress, so that Anushka would see her papa as she was used to.

The final issue that clarified itself was regarding my job, my career. A few years later, during my stint at TCS, I underwent a self-development course titled 'Who Moved My Cheese?' named after the management classic authored by Spencer Johnson. At Woodlands, I asked myself similar questions:

— Am I feeling fulfilled where I am?

— Am I realizing my full potential?

— Do I need to expand my horizons?

The answers I started getting, clearly pointed to the need for a significant change. It required me to move out of my comfort zone into hitherto uncharted waters. Looking back, I must confess that change has been good for me, the initial spells of working in new organisations and environments notwithstanding.

Harsha – Friends are forever (Mar 2001)

This memorable episode took place in early 2001, soon after I had settled into my new job at TCS. People around me had become well aware of my love for sports (the armchair variety, where you make yourself comfortable with a mug of coffee and a bowl of munchies, admiring Pete Sampras hurl down aces like greased lightning and Michael Schumacher taking on hair pin bends with barely a twitch) and quizzing.

A friend of mine mentioned to me that a sports quiz would be held at Oberoi Grand, with the quiz master being somebody called Harsha Bhogle. Hey, wasn't he your classmate? Well, not exactly; he was a year junior but that is splitting hairs. In fact, his cousin, Shrikant Joshi, too is a close friend of mine, and my classmate.

Anyway, armed with this piece of information, I made my way to the Oberoi and there, I saw Harsha, surrounded by his admirers. By this time, he had become a well-known face on TV and print media; he was the voice and face of Indian cricket to many. Hesitantly, I walked up to him and mumbled "Harsha, I wonder if you remember me, I used to be a year senior in school ... (after all, it was now twenty-five years since, and even if he had not become the hot shot media star, that's a long time for someone to remember you).

Instead, what I got was a loud, super enthusiastic shout that blasted across the hotel lobby "Where have been, my man? Hello, Debu, where have you been all these years?" I was so touched by the extraordinary gesture of warmth, by this unbelievable demonstration of being grounded and unaffected by fame and fortune, that I became speechless. One warm hug followed another, and then it was time for the show to get on the road.

During the quiz itself, I was part of the audience, as it was an impromptu decision to attend the event, to say "Hello" to an old friend. Suddenly, a question was thrown open to the audience (Who scored the slowest century in Test cricket?). Knowing the answer (Mudassar Nazar), I raised my hand and expected to get a polite round of applause from the crowd along with a trinket from Harsha. I was so very mistaken.

As soon as I answered, Harsha announced to all present, "Today is one of the happiest days of my life. Today, I have met one of my dearest friends from school, somebody with whom I go back 30 years. Debu, please come and join me on the stage." Coming on top of what had happened a few minutes back, it was too much for me to take, and my eyes just welled over.

Life carries us to widely different peaks and troughs, and far too often this difference in heights reached translates to weak memories and cursory acknowledgements. Here was this media star, making a public acknowledgement of his friendship with a school friend, going back three decades.

Do these things happen, in real life? Sometimes, they do. What more can I say, except, God bless you, dear Harsha? As long as there are people like you around, we will never be able to give up on humanity.

Chotloo – From here to eternity (Mar 2002)

The first half of 2002. It was the best of times; it was the worst of times. It was a six-month period that changed my life, and I feel, the lives of people close to me as well.

Early in the year, the TCS Utility group was absolutely euphoric after bagging the biggest deal in its history. In fact, it was one of the biggest deals to have been bagged by TCS Calcutta. United Utilities, one of the largest multi-utility organisations in the United Kingdom, had decided to outsource a wide range of services ranging from application development & maintenance to infrastructure support, on a long-term basis to TCS, with Calcutta being the primary offshore development centre.

This meant that some of us would need to relocate to UK, on a medium to long-term basis, to help things get underway. Amongst those chosen for this onsite assignment was yours truly. As you can imagine, our happiness and excitement knew no bounds. For one, it meant that we would be spreading our wings beyond national boundaries and going to the other side of the customs & immigration desk that, so far, we had seen only from the departure lounge of various airports.

More importantly, it would give us a scope to showcase our professional abilities on a global scale and prove that our much-vaunted offerings were not limited to just fanciful presentations and tall claims. The time had come to prove our mettle.

Prior to any long-term overseas assignment, all TCS employees are required, as a measure of abundant precaution, to undergo a comprehensive medical check-up along with all the family members accompanying him. In early March, Koli, Chiki and I trooped in to Wockhardt Medical Centre for a battery of tests to be carried out. We were told that the results would be forwarded to TCS in due course.

As I have mentioned elsewhere, I had suffered a heart attack in December 1999 and was more than a little concerned about the results of these tests. In due course, my fears were confirmed and the results revealed that there were certain abnormalities in my heart. It was advised that my trip should be deferred till further tests are carried out and remedial measures, as required, are undertaken.

Bitterly disappointed at being denied the chance of an international trip, having come so close, I proceeded towards my tests at RN Tagore Institute of Cardiac Sciences. Even before the doctor could formally communicate the angiography results to me, it was clear from his face that he did not have good tidings. Yes, he confirmed that I had life-threatening blockages in three of the major cardiac arteries. To quote him, "You are sitting on a virtual time bomb".

It was not a question of whether an open-heart surgery was required. It was not even a question of when. It was just a question of how soon could the arrangements be made, as every day mattered.

Mentally, I was prepared that something may need to be done to address the shortcomings of my misbehaving heart. Medication? Yes. Life style changes? Definitely. But this was something totally unthinkable – an open-heart surgery with a chance that I would never ever open my eyes again, with the most exciting phase of our lives beckoning and my darling daughter being just six years old? How could this be? It was so bloody unfair. Outside the doctor's chamber, I just rested against a pillar and let the tears race each other down my eyes, silently and despairingly.

We now had but a few days to prepare for Narayana Hrudalaya, Bangalore where it was decided that the surgery would take place. Arranging for the money, booking flight tickets, synchronizing with Mejda who would be joining us from Pune; these activities took our minds off the unthinkable quite a bit, but not completely. Coming face to face with my own mortality in such an abrupt and undeniable way, triggered a reaction that was both weird and perfectly understandable, if that is indeed possible. Not being sure of how long life would continue to partner me, there was this undeniable urge to leave some more of my genes for posterity.

During this period, we had shifted to a small apartment, where Koli and I used to sleep on the floor, in the study. Driven by a primal need to procreate, I tried to convince Koli for (what could turn out to be) our last coupling, but Koli realized what was going through me, what was driving me to a state of near desperation, if not madness. Gradually, she pacified me, reassuring me that life, in all its beauty, lay ahead of us. We needed to have faith in the Almighty and His infinite powers, and all would be well.

By His grace and mercy, things have turned out for the best. Our faith in the Almighty, which had taken a battering, was restored.

Family – Flight of Terror (Apr 2002)

A huge weight had been lifted off the family. Dr. Devi Shetty and his amazing team of cardio-thoracic surgeons, anesthetists and all had not only performed a triple-bypass surgery on me, their meticulous post-operative care had progressed me to a position where I was ready to fly back to Calcutta within eight days of the surgery and resume my life's journey.

The Bangalore-Calcutta journey was a hopping flight, with a brief halt at Hyderabad. Having seen off Mejda at Bangalore airport, we were happy that all the stages of my treatment had gone off so well (the surgery, the post-operative convalescence, regaining full lung power and everything else). The first leg of the journey was uneventful, and we were looking forward to getting back home for an early dinner.

As the aircraft took off at Hyderabad, I looked back wistfully towards my alma mater, Hyderabad Public School, fondly recalling the wonderful time I had there and the amazing friends and teachers that I had the good fortune of being associated with. These thoughts kept my mind occupied, along with on-flight chatter with Koli, Mamoni and Chiki. After the snacks tray was cleared, we were now set for the last leg of the journey, the landing at Calcutta airport.

As we approached Calcutta, the sky started to become distinctly cloudy and the flight turned a little bumpy. There was nothing unusual about that, at least till that point of time. Shortly thereafter, the pilot asked all passengers to fasten the seatbelts, as turbulent weather was expected as we got closer to Calcutta. The instability was now distinctly noticeable, if not a little disconcerting to a few fidgety passengers (please count me in that list).

People started giving nervous glances, first to their friends and family, and then all over. There was a little girl who was travelling unaccompanied; she was being paid a lot of attention and being distracted with chocolates and biscuits. It seemed to be working for a while. Then, the aircraft suddenly lurched on its side.

Immediately, any pretense of smiles and composure left the faces of all passengers and crew alike. The air-hostesses somehow managed to stay on their feet and buckled themselves in. The little girl looked dazed, wondering why all the aunties with chocolates and other goodies had suddenly disappeared.

Mamoni, by now, had taken on her stern and stony look, the crisis look, while Koli was desperately seeking divine assistance from the Almighty, firmly clasping the cross in one hand and my arm in the other. Chiki was blissfully unaware of, or unconcerned, at what was happening; being too young to know the meaning of fear does have its advantages.

Talking of myself, please remember that I had my rib cage cut open with an electric saw, and then stitched together with silver wire, less than two hundred hours back. Even on the hospital bed, the slightest coughing or sneezing would put me in agonising pain as the raw and nerve-rich ends of the ribs rubbed against each other. The pain I was feeling now was on another planetary level altogether.

As time passed, things only got worse. We were caught in a really bad norwester (a typical pre-monsoon storm, common in tropical areas) over the skies of Calcutta. You would have expected the pilots to divert the flight to a nearby airport, say Bhubaneswar, but for some reason, they chose to forego this option. Not once but twice they tried to land the aircraft, and on both the occasions they were forced to abort it due to the strong winds that were crisscrossing the fuselage. It was now more than an hour that we were hovering over Calcutta. People, who had come to the airport to receive us, were totally in the dark. One hour back, the expected time of arrival had flashed on the large screen, but there was no update thereafter. Panic had set in, especially as the staff at the airline counter refused to issue any updates or even inform the whereabouts of the aircraft.

Finally, on the third attempt, the pilots managed to land the aircraft safely. All the passengers and crew spontaneously started clapping and cheering the end of a most traumatic hour, as well as the skill of the pilots. Many amongst us, I am sure, feared the worst; I know that I definitely did! When we disembarked, it was raining outside. As we were not connected to the aerobridge, this meant that the strong winds caused many of us to get drenched, but nobody cared. **The relief on everybody's face, without exception, was ample testimony to what we had just been through.**

As Koli puts it, those whom He protects, nobody can harm.

Chotloo, Koli & Anushka – 1st international trip (Jul 2002)

After having gone through a seemingly endless series of false starts, here we were on the afternoon of 27th July, 2002 at the departure lounge of Calcutta Airport, all set to cross the boundaries of India, into totally unknown territory. Koli, Chiki and I were about to head to Warrington, United Kingdom.

174

It is difficult to describe the sense of euphoria that we felt, as we headed to the Bombay counter of Jet Airways. In the preceding few months, we had experienced the wonderful feeling of being selected by TCS for a long-term onsite assignment, only to be followed by the acute disappointment of having it deferred due to abnormalities being detected in my heart. Then, there was the terror of squaring up to the challenges of an open-heart surgery, followed by the huge relief when everything went well, in fact better than expected.

At Bombay, we were put up in Juhu Centaur for the night by Air India. I had requested my dear friend Mithu to come over to the hotel along with her husband, Siddharth (Sid) and daughter, Sumati (Sumi). We had a great time chatting for hours together while the youngsters kept themselves busy playing with a kitchen set that Sumi had got for Chiki, as a going away gift.

The next morning, we got up early. Although I had set the alarm for four a.m., it was not required. All three of us were so excited, that our body clocks were enough. After a cup of tea and biscuits, we headed to the airport. Out there, while we were waiting in line, there was a young couple, Debabrata and Shyamali Kar, who were struggling to check in, as one of the luggage pieces was an outsized bag. Being in no hurry whatsoever, we patiently stood and waited till their issues got resolved. Debabrata and Shyamali became close to us and we hope to catch up with them soon.

As we were about to board the aircraft, a member of the airline staff informed us that we had been upgraded to Business Class. We are not sure how this happened, but I suspect that the time taken waiting behind Debabrata meant that all Economy seats were allocated by the time we reached the check-in counter. Thank you, Shyamali and Debabrata, coupled with the delightful practice of overbooking, if that was indeed the case. This was a pleasant surprise for us; now we would have the luxury of extra-wide seats and gourmet meals. We saw it as an auspicious sign of things to come, and time has not proved us wrong.

As the plane took off into the skies above, we had a wonderful view of what lay below, as it was a day flight and virtually cloudless all the way from Bombay to Heathrow. From the greens of Maharashtra to the desert of the Middle East (little did I know then that a large part of my life would be spent out there, somewhere), from the Black Sea to the English Channel. It was as if all that I had read in my geography books in school had leapt out of the pages to look me in the eye.

Finally, we commenced our descent into Heathrow, the gateway to the eternal city of London, which surely, was the centre of the civilized world. Having spent my childhood in an English township, Digboi, I had always been fascinated by English history, from King Alfred and the burning cakes to Winston Churchill's blood, sweat and tears. To stand on English soil, raised goose bumps on my forearm, I kid you not. After going through immigration and other formalities, each of which made me tense and excited simultaneously, it was time for a short flight that was as quaint as it was enjoyable. Straight from an Air India Jumbo 747 to a tiny British Midlands aircraft (I forget the model number), from cruising at 36,000 feet to flying barely above the ground, from elaborate three-course meals to a cup of tea and muffins, the change was enough to make you realize that you were almost there. The countryside below looked so geometrically precise and green, it felt as if you could smell the meadows and caress the grazing sheep.

Finally, we started the last leg of our journey, a ride in a black cab from Manchester airport to Warrington. A journey, that had begun from our flat in Jodhpur Park and would end in an hour or so, in the bed & breakfast establishment of Arthur and Beryl Cunningham. What I remember most vividly about this drive was the realization that green, as a colour, could have so many distinct hues. Light green, dark green, blackish green, yellowish green and many more. Looking above, it was as if a hundred pencils with sharp tips, had scratched the surface of the sky, the scratches being the jet trails of aircrafts. In the polluted skies of India, I had never seen anything like it and this fascinated me. Around ten p.m., the taxi pulled into Arthur's B&B and our journey was complete.

A new chapter in our lives had begun.

Anushka – A birthday party (Dec 2002)

10th December is always a special day for Aditi and me. As it is for our little darling princess, Anushka aka Chiki. After all, it is her birthday. 2002 was going to be no different. So, what if it was going to be celebrated in our home away from home, in faraway Warrington?

While preparing the list of invitees, we started with the usual suspects; our close friends, people who regularly invited us for dinners and get together parties and of course, those who had invited us for their children's birthday parties. Then, there were a few friends, and of course the big boss and his deputy, who were based out of Manchester, just about twenty miles from Warrington. How could we leave out the bachelors in our team; after all they hardly got to eat quality home-made food except on the rare occasion. So, the list kept on growing, to be honest, even without our realizing to what extent. Every day, I would come back home and somehow mutter to Aditi that the list had become longer, till the number of eighty was finally reached. Or was it breached? I really do not remember.

The evening before, we knew that we had dug quite a big hole for ourselves.

As Aditi had planned to serve mostly home-cooked delicacies, we were now talking about a serious amount of cooking to be done, not to speak of prepping, serving and cleaning. There was also the question of space to be considered as our house was a reasonably sized two-bedroomed town house, not a spacious mansion that could accommodate eighty to ninety persons at one go. In an effort to manage the show, we requested the bachelors to come early in the evening, with the families to come later (By which time, we expected, or rather hoped, that the bachelors would have departed). Oh! How naïve and wishful our thinking was!

On the cooking front, two of our friends, Joyjit and Rupa, kindly took some of the load on their own shoulders, without us having to request them. The whole evening and night prior to the big day, Aditi kept on prepping and cooking food.

On the day itself, as our guests started coming in, we realized the sheer magnitude of the invitation list. Eighty doesn't sound like a lot, except when they do start coming in and occupying the chairs; now that's something that I would leave to the readers' imagination. When the bachelors continue to hang around while the family units start to arrive, then you hit the panic button. Things reached a stage that there were not enough chairs or even sitting spaces around. People started to sit on the stair case, the beds and wherever they could. The sight had to be seen to be believed.

When all was said and done, you had not only the three of us who were too tired to raise a finger, but many of our dear friends as well who had pitched in manfully. Without their incredible support, I shudder to think of what could have been.

All said and done, it was a birthday party not to be forgotten easily.

Closing Thoughts – Debasish (Chotloo)

Having come so far, having traversed a journey with more than its fair share of crests and troughs, of joys and tears, it is indeed tempting to ask, as Oliver Twist did, "May I have some more, please?". As somebody who has been privileged to have been taken through as exhaustive and comprehensive a journey of life that you can hope for, and then some more, I have tried to put together a 360° view of what life and Father Time have showered on my family and me.

A lot more remains unsaid, implicitly and explicitly.

I would like to thank each and every one of you for being my co-traveler in life. If, somewhere along the journey, my thoughts have been able to strike a chord in your hearts, or resonate with your experiences and feelings, I shall consider myself to be that much more enriched and grateful.

Before winding down, I would like to leave you with a couple of closing thoughts, especially for those who may either have made it big in your lives, or for those who feel that they have been singled out by Fate rather unfairly.

Empathy

By the grace of the Almighty, prosperity has visited some of our lives, while others may have been somewhat overlooked. While we, the fortunate few, would like to believe this was the consequence of hard work, smart minds and carefully thought-out choices on the road called life, a tiny voice within me keeps trying to make itself heard "Do not forget the hand of luck and God." Maybe, one is but another name for the other.

During the mid-seventies, I heard a song that remains etched in my heart, a song that was originally written and sung by Phil Ochs. Joan Baez later did a cover (the version that I fell in love with), the words of the first stanza of which go as follows:

Show me a prison, show me a jail,

Show me a prisoner whose face has gone pale

And I'll show you, young man, with so many reasons why

There but for fortune, go you or I

Father Time has taken us, friends and brothers, along different paths. Yes, we have made our choices; what do we cling to, what do we give up? Do we choose the comfort of a familiar home over the challenges of unknown frontiers? Do we value the loving arms of a parent over the exciting call of the wild? Do factors influencing our lives, education and jobs play out in our favour or not? Did we opt for bravado over the grind that endears you to your bosses? Perhaps yes, perhaps no.

Regardless of how we responded to the various questions asked by life, we have had chances to look back and see where the tides of time have carried us. We may or may not like what we see; our hearts may be filled with joy, pride or regret. I have but one appeal; please let us not puff our chest so large that we fail to empathise with those whose journey has not been as fortunate and blessed as ours have been.

If we can help them, in any meaningful way, please let us extend our hands in love, in brotherhood for no man ever became weaker by reaching out. If we can and choose not to, then let us at least hang our heads down in shame.

Count your blessings

I complained that I had no shoes until I met a man who had no feet – Old Chinese proverb.

This was the text written on a beautiful wall hanging that I remember from Sandy Aunty's drawing room, seen many eons ago. Somehow, these words have been imprinted on my mind. It is easy for us to complain and endlessly keep carping on how Dame Fortune has given us the short shrift in so many ways.

If I look back to my family, my classmates and colleagues, it is easy for me to identify those that have moved far ahead in life. While some occupy corner offices in multi-national corporations, others have become business barons and industrial tycoons. High government officials, financial wizards; the list goes on and on. Not being a member of any of these privileged groups, it is only fair to say that somewhere down the road, life has treated me unfairly; that I should wait for my turn and ask Him, whenever I do meet Him, why I did not receive His infinite generosity as others have.

Right? Absolutely wrong.

Life is like a pyramid and that is an undeniable fact. Look around you and you will find many instances of your peers and relatives, who were similarly placed as you were at a point of time, but are facing life's struggles and challenges with considerably more difficulty today. On the Internet, many applications are available that, based on your income and wealth, rank you amongst the world's wealthiest. Most of us, including you, dear reader, will rank right up there, in or near the topmost layers. If that be so, how do you consider yourself to be unfortunate?

Moving away from money matters, do we even realize how fortunate we are to be living in an environment where freedom of speech is taken for granted, where the law of the land is more than just empty words? Regardless of where most of us live, we are protected by defense forces that put their lives on the line to ensure our sound sleep; we are fed by farmers and peasants who toil day and night.

Complaining is easy, acknowledging the blood, sweat and tears of the millions who have made our life possible is a little less so.

Review Comments

(Just a handful of oh, so many... You have overwhelmed us with your kind words and effusive praise)

Sunita Maheshwari

A fascinating memoir that spans cities, generations, heartbreaks, love and hope. Debasish Ghosh aka Chotloo brings the India of the 50s and beyond alive with his stories of family, friends and people. He weaves through his memories like the events happened yesterday – vivid, lucid and insightful. Chotloo has used his life's bitter-sweet experiences to acknowledge relationships and share learnings. He leaves us with two key learnings at the end of the book 'A backward glance – at life'; stay empathetic and count one's blessings, always.

Ajita Sircar

It was an absolutely gripping read. Your lucid and articulate style of writing is indeed appealing. I loved the introduction of the memoir, where you have subtly interwoven the laws of science to the laws of human understanding.

The portrayal of your family background set against the backdrop of India's independence and growth is truly remarkable. The recollections of your childhood days are not only heart-warming but also poignant and soul stirring. Your graphic narrative also reflects your philosophical bent of mind and your chronicle depicts your true understanding of human relationships and human nature.

The autobiography highlights your noble character revealing the fact that at the core of your heart you are a true gentleman as you have been honest and explicit in your portrayal.

Shilpi Chawla Bhardwaj

Amazing. I actually read a few pages more than once to completely understand it. Your understanding of relationships and articulation is commendable. I want to go through each and every phrase and emotion attached to it. Every pain gives us a lesson, and every lesson makes us wiser than yesterday.

Puneet Gupta

It's so splendid. We are reading it at our pace. Every alternate day, we discuss your roller coaster life and compare it with our dull lives. Your writing style is very impressive ... your name should be Debasish Tharoor. It's something that I feel like reading again and again, a few pages at a time and then ponder over it. There are serious lessons to be learnt about how to love selflessly, sacrifices we need to make in life and invest in building relations.

Prasad Indraganti

It is fantastic. You have wonderful style and used it the best way. It is very delicious. It is a day's meal from morning coffee to an evening dinner. You have a solid English expression and the art of articulation. Characters come out alive in flesh and blood.

Gargee Chakravarty

I am drowning in nostalgia, thanks to your journal. All I can say at this point, is, you do have the gift of expressing yourself incredibly well. Very thought provoking. Did not know that you have spent the earliest part of your life in Ghatshila. I have very good memories of this little township as it was eons ago.

Feels like you're sitting right here and telling me this story. That is a very rare quality of writing. So far, I am in love with your Mamoni. An ardent request – please write a separate book on her please.

Shankar Ghosh

So beautifully written could not stop sharing. Was just reading it non-stop from morning; trust me its gripping.

Panchali Ganguly

You have a skill and particular style of clear thought process. A lot of anecdotes I already knew, I guess that's how close we are as buddies. Some I was part of ... picnic on asbestos, hop scotch games etc.

Pankaja Srinivasan

It was like walking behind you as you told your story. And what made it extra special for me was how so many people that you mention, I know them too.

Mousumi Ghosh

Have read the latest version and enjoyed it. Great continuity. Captivating to say the least. Proud for you being so daringly honest.

Sharmila Mitra

I was going through it in segments. Really liked it, as I could relate to some of the incidents. For me too, it was going down the memory lane. Your command over the language is really good. In fact, I just wanted to request you that there are people like me who are not so good. For us, if you could just simplify your expressions a little. Besides, it is too long for me to finish reading fast. But overall, I have to appreciate your effort. I will keep you posted as I keep going through it further.

Prasenjit Gupta

Thank you for sharing these memories. They were a fascinating read – I did not know anything about the major upheavals in your life.

The manuscript is very well written and makes for fascinating reading. It certainly is a delightful read as it stands. It would be lovely to have it published so you could distribute it to your friends and family. I'm sure that they would appreciate that, and it would be a valuable record for your daughter – and her children when she has a family of her own.

Toopsi Ray

I did enjoy reading it. I am filled with admiration with how honest you have been. This is, after all, your point of view. That's not easy. I laughed at all your memories and they are great memories to have. Showed me a story I had no idea of. I identified with some aspects of Jharna Pishi.

If it's ok with you, at some point, I would like my girls to read it!

It's a great thing to leave for your daughter. The girls have been telling me for years to write down my story just for them. Reading yours, I might just get down to it.

Ratnabali Bose

Bravo, Chotloo! Proud of you. Even if I had not known any of the people here, it was hugely absorbing and very well written. You have, in a simple frank and lucid manner encapsulated all those years in such an interesting way. For me, it brings back great memories and also, I now know so much more about my family. I am so happy that you have taken this effort. I was hell bent on finishing, and was utterly fascinated and moved.

Debjani Chatterjee

I came to know a lot more about you as a human being and my respect for you and Boudi have gone up manifold. And I would have loved to meet your enigmatic mother in person. Actually speaking, I am too overwhelmed by the varied experiences you have had and so, it is difficult to give my views in an unbiased manner.

Acknowledgements

This has been a humble and intensely personal attempt to put down on paper, a sprinkling of life's most vivid memories and valued lessons of life, as seen through our eyes, rose-tinted or jaundiced, we do not know. We have tried to make it as honest as we could, but it is only fair to say that personal prejudices and memory lapses are bound to have their presence felt along the way, somewhere down the line.

First and foremost, we need to doff my hat to our dear Boudi (Mousumi Ghosh) and Koli (Aditi Ghosh) whose vivid recollection of people and events, of locations and environments, is nothing less than mind blowing. The flux of time, all of half a century and more, has not in any way affected the clarity of the days gone by. We guess that it is as much a reflection of the unique journey that life has taken us on, as it is of our remarkable memories and the deep impact various chapters of time have left on our collective minds and psyches.

On this journey, it would be churlish if we did not make mention of the following persons who have helped us to transform a hazy idea into something far more tangible. They include the following (if we have inadvertently missed somebody, please forgive us, for we are known to be forgetful, even in the best of times):

Abhik & Anuradha Bhattacharya, Aditi Ghosh, Ajita Sircar, Apu Ganguly, Arijit Roy, Badr A. Aldawssary, Debjani Chatterjee, H. Krishna Reddy, Gargee Chakravorty, Haimanti Chakraborty, Hansa Piparsania, Indrani Roychowdhury, Jitender Singh Kanwar, Kalpana Sinha, Mayura Chandra,

189

Mousumi Ghosh, Munjal Mehta, Pankaja Srinivasan, Prasad and Madhavi Indragunti, Puneet Gupta, Ratnabali Bose, Runa Chatterjee, Rupa Ghosh, Sandip Lahiri, Sandra Maheshwari, Shankar Ghosh, Shilpi Chawla Bhardwaj, Shubhra Gupta, Somnath Chatterjee, Sudhir Dante, Sunita Maheshwari, Sutapa Majumdar and Toopsi Roy and many others, our well-wishers, and most importantly, every one of you who have contributed to making our lives worth remembering, worth recounting.

**God bless all of you. Stay in peace
May the light of the Almighty always shine bright
in all your lives.**

Lightning Source UK Ltd.
Milton Keynes UK
UKHW010931060223
416537UK00002B/603

9 798887 049793